A YOUNG MANX HISTORY

Sara Goodwins

Loaghtan Books
Caardee
Dreemskerry Hill
Maughold
Isle of Man
IM7 1BE

Published by Loaghtan Books

First published: September 2015

Copyright © Sara Goodwins, 2015

Typesetting and origination by:
Loaghtan Books

Printed and bound by:
Lavenham Press

Website: www.loaghtanbooks.com

ISBN: 978 1 908060 13 6

All rights reserved. No part of this publication may be reproduced, stored on a retrieval system or transmitted in any form or by any means without prior permission of the publishers.

For Charlie Link
in the hope that one day
he will want to read it

CONTENTS

1	Early Mann	5
2	Vikings bring Tynwald	12
3	Mediaeval Mann	20
4	King... Stanley?	27
5	Making Money and Mischief	35
6	Masters and Mann	44
7	Mann today	52
	Something extra: Kings and Things	58
	Acknowledgements and selected bibliography	60

MANX NATIONAL ANTHEM   ARRANE ASHOONAGH VANNIN

O land of our birth,	O' Halloo nyn ghooie,
O gem of God's earth,	O' Ch'liegeen ny s'bwaaie
O Island so strong and so fair;	Ry gheddyn er ooir aalin Yee,
Built firm as Barrule,	Ta dt' Ardstoyl Reill Thie
Thy Throne of Home Rule	Myr Barrool er nyc hoie
Makes us free as thy sweet mountain air.	Dy reayl shin ayns seyrsnys as shee.
When Orry, the Dane,	Tra Gorree yn Dane
In Mannin did reign,	Haink er traie ec y Lhane
'Twas said he had come from above;	Son Ree Mannin v'eh er ny reih
For wisdom from Heav'n	'S va creenaght veih Heose
To him had been giv'n	Er ny chur huggey neose
To rule us with justice and love.	Dy reill harrin lesh cairys as graih.
Our fathers have told	Ren nyn ayryn g'imraa
How Saints came of old,	Va Nooghyn shenn traa
Proclaiming the Gospel of Peace;	Yn Sushtal dy Hee fockley magh
That sinful desires,	Shegin yeearree peccoil
Like false Baal fires,	Myr far aileyn Vaal,
Must die ere our troubles can cease.	Ve er ny chur mow son dy bragh.
Ye sons of the soil,	Vec ooasle yn Theihll
In hardship and toil,	Ayns creoighys tooilleil
That plough both the land and the sea,	Ta traaue ooir as faarkey, Gow cree
Take heart while you can,	Ny jarrood yn fer mie
And think of the Man	Ta coadey 'n lught-thie
Who toiled by the Lake Galilee.	Ren tooilleil liorish Logh Galilee.
When fierce tempests smote	D'eiyr yn sterrm noon as noal
That frail little boat,	Yn baatey beg moal
They ceased at His gentle command;	Fo-harey hug Eh geay as keayn
Despite all our fear,	Trooid ooilley nyn ghaue
The Saviour is near	Ta'n Saualtagh ec laue
To safeguard our dear Fatherland.	Dy choadey nyn Vannin veg veen.
Let storm-winds rejoice,	Lhig dorrinyn bra
And lift up their voice,	Troggal seose nyn goraa
No danger our homes can befall;	As brishey magh ayns ard arrane
Our green hills and rocks	Ta nyn groink aalin glass
Encircle our flocks,	Yn vooir cummal ass
And keep out the sea like a wall.	As coadey lught-thie as shioltane.
Our Island, thus blest, No foe can molest;	Nyn Ellan fo-hee
Our grain and our fish shall increase;	Cha boir noidyn ee
From battle and sword Protecteth the Lord,	Dy bishee nyn eeastyn as grain
And crowneth our nation with peace.	Nee'n Chiarn shin y reayll
	Voish strieughyn yn theihll
	As crooinnagh lesh shee 'n ashoon ain.
Then let us rejoice	Lhig dooin boggoil bee,
With heart, soul and voice,	Lesh annym as cree,
And in The Lord's promise confide;	As croghey er gialdyn yn Chiarn;
That each single hour	Dy vodmayd dagh oor,
We trust in His power,	Treish teil er e phooar,
No evil our souls can betide.	Dagh olk ass nyn anmeenyn 'hayrn.

CHAPTER 1

EARLY MANN

In the beginning

Did you know that land moves? Of course you did. You've seen pictures of volcanoes and mudslides, which is land getting excited and whizzing around quickly. But land also moves very slowly. The Isle of Man, for example, is moving at about two centimetres per year closer to England. That's about the same speed as your fingernails grow.

Ever been to Australia? No? The Isle of Man has! Or rather it's come back from near there. It took its time though. About 500 million years ago, which is so long ago it's almost beyond imagining, the lump of land which became the Isle of Man was quite a long way south of Australia. Very gradually it drifted northwards. As it journeyed lots of things happened to the land and created all the different sorts of rock which you can see around the island today. The limestone used to build Castle Rushen, for example, is made out of the shells of sea animals which lived in the sea when the island was passing the equator. As the land moved it also collided with other bits of land which were drifting in different directions and the edges of the land which bumped together got a bit crumpled. You can see this at places such as the Marine Drive.

Once the Isle of Man got to where it is now, it wasn't quite the shape it is today. The flattish bit of the island at the northern end was missing. About two million years ago – quite recently in the life of the island, but still a very long time ago – the world got very much colder. Ice from the north pole covered the Isle of Man, Scotland, most of Wales and Ireland and went to about half way down England. During warm spells, which could last thousands of years, the ice melted and the land poked through. Then the world got cold again and the ice came back.

As the ice moved backwards and forwards from the north it scraped the top soil and rocks off land near the north pole and pushed all the rubble south. When the ice melted it left the soil behind. You've seen how, in the sea, waves leave flotsam on a beach when the tide goes out; the ice did the same with all the bits of rock and earth it had picked up, dropping them behind it as it melted. The land around Bride and Andreas was pushed there by frozen rivers called glaciers, which is how the Isle of Man got to be the shape it is.

Mann is south of Cape Horn
500 million BC

Mann becomes an island
10,000 BC

How to make an island

Not that the Isle of Man was an island yet. You've probably looked out to sea on a bright sunny day and seen Scotland, England, Ireland or Wales on the other side of the water. What you may not have thought about is that all the land joins up under the sea. About 20,000 years ago, the sea wasn't there, so valleys connected all the different parts of the British Isles and Europe – they are sometimes called a 'land bridge'. The very first people to visit Mann probably walked here looking for food.

It was really the ending of the Ice Age which turned Mann into an island. When the world got warmer and the ice melted, all that water had to go somewhere, so it filled up the valleys between the higher bits of land. The middle bit of the Isle of Man is really the tops of mountains surrounded by water.

Mountain peaks are usually cold and bare, and that's what the new island was like at first. Gradually seeds were blown here or dropped by birds, and plants began to grow. In time, trees covered most of the island, and birds and animals also moved in. Birds and insects with wings got here by flying or being blown by the wind. Small animals and other insects probably floated here clinging to twigs and branches brought by the sea. The Isle of Man has no native large wild animals like deer or foxes precisely because it is an island and they can't easily get here.

Moving in

People could though. Around 9,000 years ago, people came to live on the island, paddling across the sea in dug-out canoes. We're not sure why they came. Perhaps they were looking for food or a good place to live. Perhaps they were fishing and got caught in a storm. Perhaps they were merely curious about the lonely land they could see across the sea. Anyway, they came – and stayed.

These people from long ago didn't build permanent places to live, but moved around a lot according to what was most comfortable in the different seasons. People who travel around like this are called nomads. They made tents out of animal skins and ate whatever they could find or catch, which is why these sorts of nomads are often called hunter-gatherers. They also used flint to make knives and axes, so this part of history is sometimes called the Stone Age.

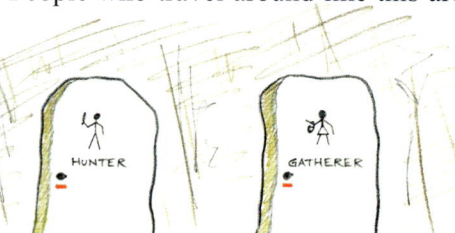

Stories say that the giant Finn MacCooil made the Isle of Man by scooping up a handful of earth from Ireland and throwing it at a rival giant. Finn missed. It went splosh into the Irish Sea and created the Isle of Man. The hole left in Ireland filled with water and became Lough Neagh, the third largest lake in Europe.

People first live on Mann — 7,000 BC

Start of Stone Age — 4,000 BC

Gradually people realised that they would be less likely to go hungry if they grew the food they needed rather than relying on being able to find it. They therefore started to plant crops and keep animals. Growing your own food means of course that you have to wait while plants grow, so people stopped moving around and lived in one place more or less all the time. They had invented farming. People had already tamed dogs to help with hunting, but when they began to stay in one place they also tamed animals like pigs, sheep and cows. Manx Loaghtan sheep today look very much like Stone Age sheep did then.

DID YOU KNOW?

After dogs, the next animals to be tamed were probably pigs.

The new farmers didn't travel around so much, so no longer needed to make their houses light enough to carry. They therefore they stopped living in tents, which could blow away or get damaged, and started building houses of wood and stone with thatched roofs. What was left of a Stone Age house was found at Ronaldsway when the aerodrome was being built.

As well as building permanent homes, Stone Age people also built permanent religious structures. We can't call them churches because we don't know what these very early Manxmen believed in, but their religious buildings seem to be a mix of burial ground and somewhere they worshipped their gods. Three of the most famous places like this on the Isle of Man are Cashtal-yn-Ard, King Orry's Grave (nothing to do with King Orry – sorry) and the Meayll Circle. The last is very unusual as the burials are arranged in a circle and nothing like it has been found anywhere else.

People had stopped being nomads, but that didn't mean that they never went anywhere. You might live in a house but you still go on holiday, stay with friends, go on school trips, etc. Stone Age people also went on journeys, not just around the Isle of Man, but to friends and relations living in the lands across the sea. As a result they learned about the different ways their neighbours lived, and sometimes copied them. The same thing happens today. We wouldn't eat spaghetti if no-one had visited Italy, or write on paper if no-one had been to China.

Heavy metal!

The main change in the lives of Stone Age people is that they stopped using stone. That's not completely true. They carried on using stone for ordinary things because it was easy to find, but started making their best tools out of metal. Bronze. (It was also better for showing off with.)

Making and using bronze was quite a big change in the lives of ordinary Manx people, so this part of history is called the Bronze Age. You can get tin mines, and copper mines, but not bronze mines because bronze is an alloy, which means that it's made by mixing different metals together. Just as you might make a cake by mixing together different ingredients,

Start of Bronze Age	Cashtal yn Ard built	BBQ in use at Clay Head
2,500 BC	2,000 BC	1,500 BC

bronze is made by melting copper and tin together, with sometimes a bit of lead added to make the mixture more runny. The Manx had copper at Bradda and Langness, and people found lead all over the island, but Mann had no tin. In fact most of Europe had no tin – it is only found in Cornwall (England), Spain and Brittany.

Signs of people making bronze have been found at Ballagawne near Port St Mary, and Kiondroghad, Andreas, so the makers must have got tin from somewhere. They got it in the same way we get things that we want today. They 'bought' it. As money wasn't being used yet on the Isle of Man, the Manx bronze makers traded for their tin, i.e. they swapped something they had for the tin they wanted. The tin came from Cornwall but the Manx might not have got it from the Cornish. The Manx went backwards and forwards to Ireland a lot, and the Irish got their tin from Cornwall. Experts think that the Manx bronze makers may have done a deal with their Irish cousins for the tin they needed.

Because bronze was very expensive, things made from bronze were used as 'best'. You might have a stone axe and stone knives to use round the farm, but getting together with a rival family from the next valley meant wearing your bronze knife to show off. Your sword, if you could afford one, was also bronze. A bronze sword was found at Berrag near Sandygate and is now in the Manx Museum. It is three thousand years old.

A few people might have been making bronze on the Isle of Man, but most Manx people were farmers who also did a bit of fishing and hunting. They lived in large round houses, about the size of a netball court, with stone walls and a thatched roof. Mum and Dad, children, grandparents, aunts, uncles and cousins all lived in the same round house, with their animals. In the middle of the floor was a fire for cooking, which also kept them warm. There was no chimney, so smoke drifted out through the thatch. If the weather was good they often ate outside. Clay Head, just south of Garwick, was one of their open-air cooking sites – a sort of Bronze Age barbeque.

Building houses, particularly big ones, takes a lot of time and effort, so Bronze Age houses were used for hundreds of years. What's left of three Bronze Age round houses were found at Ballakaighen near Castletown. Like many farms today, the Ballakaighen round houses were lived in, probably by the same family, for hundreds of years. Members of that family would have seen a new metal come into fashion. Iron.

DID YOU KNOW?

Bronze is soft. Although bronze knives axes and swords look good, people used stone tools for doing the real work.

Swapping brown for grey

The Bronze Age became the Iron Age when metal workers stopped making things in bronze and started making them in iron. Iron is more difficult to work

Fort built on top of South Barrule	Start of Iron Age
1,200 BC	1,000 BC

with than bronze because it is much harder, but that made it more useful. The Isle of Man has a lot of iron ore and it can be found on the surface at Maughold, so there was no need to dig for it. Iron is an 'element', which means that it isn't mixed with anything else, so there was no need to rely on Ireland or Cornwall any more for the ingredients to make alloys like bronze.

The Manx still had a close relationship with Ireland though, and the Manx and the Irish had a similar way of life. Most people were farmers, and families tended to send one or more of their children to live in foster homes, rather like some children go to boarding school today. There were three main reasons for fostering. Firstly, children made friends with people who might be helpful when they got older. Secondly, children might be taught things which their parents didn't know and couldn't teach them. Thirdly, fostering made life more peaceful. Families would be less likely to quarrel if they were looking after each other's children. The runes on one of the crosses in Kirk Michael church say 'Mal Lumkun erected this cross in memory of Mal Mura his foster [mother]…Better it is to leave a good foster son than a bad son.'

Iron Age houses were very similar to Bronze Age houses in that they were round, made of wood or stone and had thatch or turf as a roof. What's left of Iron Age farms can be seen at Close ny Chollagh, Braust and The Braaid as well as other places around the island. In the remains of their houses, the Iron Age farming families on St Patrick's Isle left behind a very rare find. At 2,500 years old, it's the earliest human flea in Britain!

Iron Age people probably believed in gods and goddesses based on the natural world; trees and plants, etc. The people who ran the religion were called druids, who were also in charge of making sure everyone obeyed the law. Iron Age goddesses liked living in rivers, and druids held religious ceremonies among trees or by pools especially if they had waterfalls. Spooyt Vane (white spout) at the end of Glen Mooar, Inneen Vooar (big girl) in Dhoon Glen and Rhenass Waterfall in Glen Helen are thought to have been places important to druids.

Iron Age people didn't have books or paper but did write things down. They used a sort of writing called ogham, which is based on straight lines cut into twigs. Ogham is also relatively simple to cut into stone. Ogham written on a stone found

> One of the druids' gods was called Manannan and legend says that the Isle of Man was named after him. He was supposed to protect the island by covering it in fog so that its enemies couldn't see it. Even today, mist is often referred to as the cloak of Manannan.

Human flea on St Patrick's Isle

450 BC

at Ballaqueeny near Port St Mary railway station talks about 'Dovaidu son of the Druid'.

Christians come

It was during the Iron Age that Christianity arrived on Mann. Remember that the Manx were friends with people living in Ireland? The Irish were great traders and had lots of contact with other countries. The Irish also thought that learning was very important, so scholars from other countries came to use the libraries in Ireland. As a lot of people in Europe had become Christian, so they passed their beliefs on to the Irish. The Irish told the Manx and Christianity gradually began to be the main religion on Mann.

According to stories, it was St Patrick who converting Ireland to Christianity when Maughold was rude to him. As a punishment, Maughold – he wasn't a saint yet – was sent to sea in a tiny boat called a coracle, and wasn't even given any oars. The sea delivered him to the Isle of Man, and he promised to serve Patrick from then on.

Two more of St Patrick's disciples, Romulus and Conindrus, are said to have converted the Isle of Man to Christianity, but the real change over probably wasn't quite so sudden as that.

At the beginning, Christians on Mann (and in Ireland) didn't organise their churches in the same way as Christians in the rest of Europe – Britain was a bit muddled as to which version it should use and different arrangements cropped up depending on where you lived and what your local priest or bishop believed. The first churches in the Isle of Man were very small, made of earth and with only the basic four walls and a roof. The mini churches didn't have luxuries such as windows, even in the tiny room attached to them where the priest lived. They were called Cabbals and were so small that most services must have been held outside.

About a hundred years later

> **DID YOU KNOW?**
>
> St Maughold's Well or Chibbyr Vaghal marks where St Maughold first landed on Mann. It's on Maughold Head but if you go and see it, don't step back. There's an almost sheer drop to the sea!

Christianity arrives on Mann   Lonan Old Church built

447 AD   480 AD

10

> One of the most famous keeills is St Trinian at the foot of Greeba Mountain. It's got no roof because a buggane who lived in the mountain didn't like being woken up by the church bells, so came and tore the roof off.
> Several times.

the Cabbals were replaced by Keeills. Keeills were only a bit larger, but did have a window, and were built of stone. The ruins of lots of keeills can be seen all over the Isle of Man. Many parish churches are either keeills which have been made bigger, or new buildings built where a keeill once was. Old Kirk Braddan and St Runius Church, Marown, are both on the sites of old keeills.

Just as we enjoy showing off the things we like – how many of you have posters of football teams or pop stars at home? – so the new Christians wanted to show off their new religion. They did so by cutting and carving stone into crosses. Collections of these crosses can be seen around the island in the churches of Maughold, Braddan, Kirk Michael, Jurby, Andreas and Bride, for example, as well as in the Manx Museum. To start with the designs were made up of woven lines called knotwork, because it looks like rope knotted into a pattern. Then fantastic birds and animals were included in the knotwork. The cross carvers didn't invent the animals, but copied them and their stories from new and rather pushy visitors to the island.

The Vikings.

Manx crosses start to be carved

600 AD

CHAPTER 2

VIKINGS BRING TYNWALD

The Romans didn't like getting their feet wet, so the sea stopped any ideas the Romans had of invading the Isle of Man. They did get to Liverpool and Heysham, however, and probably traded with the Manx. Remember trading? That's swopping something you have for something you want. The Romans didn't like England though. They thought it cold, wet and miserable and thought that Mann might be worse. They certainly didn't want to live there. So, having been left in peace for centuries it was a bit of a shock for the Manx when the Vikings decided they were going to move in.

VENI VIDI … ABII
I came I saw … I went away

Noisy neighbours

It was 798 and the Norsemen (the word means 'men of the north') had already practised their raiding on the north-east coast of England. They were experts by the time they got to the Isle of Man.

Vikings started off by attacking the Isle of Man and stealing anything they wanted, but that wasn't their real job. Going Viking was a hobby, which they did for fun and to grab extra pocket money. Vikings were really farmers and came from a cold country, where there was no daylight in winter. The Manx farms were much better than their own – so was the weather – so the Vikings soon decided to stay on the island.

SUMMER IN NORWAY

SUMMER IN THE ISLE OF MAN

Vikings attack St Patrick's Isle
Calf of Man crucifixion stone carved
Balladoole ship burial

798   800   900

> **DID YOU KNOW?**
>
> Vikings who died in bed rather than by fighting went to a special afterlife called Niflheim where it was always foggy.

Besides, the Isle of Man was a very good base from which to raid the lands around it, and Vikings were great with boats.

Viking boats are called longships because, guess what!, they're long! The longships had sails for travelling across the sea, and oars for going up rivers and for extra speed. They weren't comfortable though. Viking longships had no cabin of any sort and the crew slept in the bottom of the boat or on the rowing benches. If it rained or was stormy, everyone got wet.

We know about the size and shape of Viking ships because important leaders were sometimes buried in their boat. One ship burial was found at Balladoole just west of Castletown, and the outline of the boat is marked with stones.

Viking way of life

Vikings loved fighting and thought that peace was for sissies.

Peace didn't really fit into the Viking's way of doing things. They liked nothing better than a good scrap and enjoyed boasting about how brave they were. Boys were taught how to fight, and men were expected to own and carry weapons to show off how fierce and rich they were. Despite the pictures, Vikings didn't wear helmets with horns though – they get caught on things.

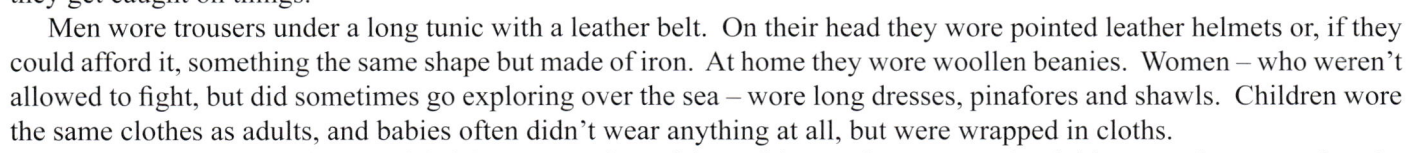

Men wore trousers under a long tunic with a leather belt. On their head they wore pointed leather helmets or, if they could afford it, something the same shape but made of iron. At home they wore woollen beanies. Women – who weren't allowed to fight, but did sometimes go exploring over the sea – wore long dresses, pinafores and shawls. Children wore the same clothes as adults, and babies often didn't wear anything at all, but were wrapped in cloths.

Being very good at sailing and fighting meant that Vikings didn't make very good neighbours. They moved to the Isle of Man and made it very clear that they were now in charge.

Even so, that didn't mean that they were always at war with the people who were here first. You can see what's left of a thousand-year-old farm at The Braaid, Marown. Vikings preferred oblong houses to the round ones the Celts built. At The Braaid a Celtic round house stands next to a couple of Viking longhouses, and experts think that people were living in both sorts at the same time. Many Vikings married girls from local Celtic families and probably bossed their new relations around. You might argue with people living on the same farm, but you're highly unlikely to try to kill them!

Round Tower built on St Patrick's Isle
920

Pagan Lady buried on St Patrick's Isle
950

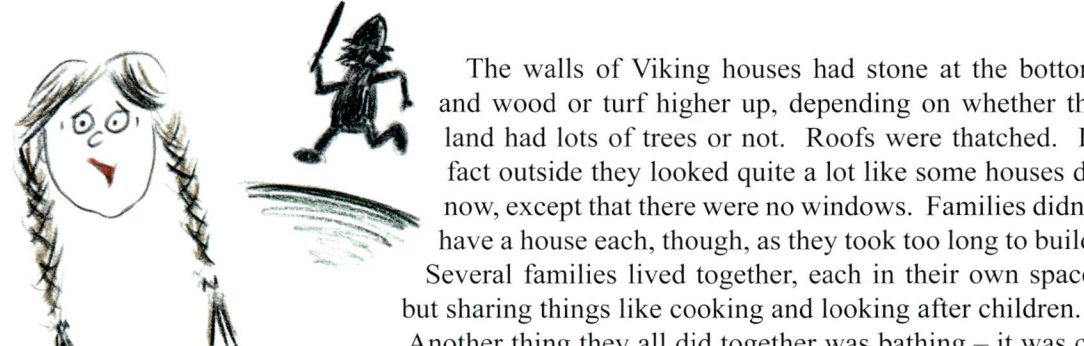

The walls of Viking houses had stone at the bottom and wood or turf higher up, depending on whether the land had lots of trees or not. Roofs were thatched. In fact outside they looked quite a lot like some houses do now, except that there were no windows. Families didn't have a house each, though, as they took too long to build. Several families lived together, each in their own space, but sharing things like cooking and looking after children.

Another thing they all did together was bathing – it was considered a great way to meet people. Vikings liked being clean, washed every day and had a bath about once a week. They also had their own combs usually made out of bone. Men carried their combs in a stiff case made of antler or bone to protect the comb's teeth, while women carried theirs in a cloth bag. Clothes didn't have pockets, but people usually had a small bag hung from their belt.

> **DID YOU KNOW?**
>
> A Viking bride was often given a cat as a wedding present. Pest control!

Looking good

Rather like famous footballers today, Vikings loved looking good. Men and women both wore bracelets and brooches, and men liked wearing torcs, which are large metal rings worn around the neck. Women fastened their pinafores with two large oval brooches, one below each shoulder and often wore beads strung between the two brooches. Beads were sometimes used as trading tokens, or a kind of money; you could swop something for a bead and then swop that bead for something else. The grave of an important Viking lady, now called The Pagan Lady, was found on St Patrick's Isle and it contained seventy three different beads. She was very rich.

Most people at the time didn't think that slavery was wrong, and Vikings often captured people to keep as slaves. When important Vikings died they were often buried with things they had owned which they liked or which showed how important they were. Slaves were owned and so could be buried with their dead masters. A slave girl was buried in her master's ship at Balladoole and another with her master in the Viking grave at Ballateare.

Viking graves, or rather the crosses which were put up to mark where the graves were, are one of the main things which show how important the Isle of Man was to Vikings. We even know what some of the Vikings who lived on the Isle of Man were called, because of writing on the crosses. The Thorwald cross in St Andrew's Church,

> Everybody had long hair except slaves. Slaves had to have short hair and also had to wear a thrall ring, which looked like a dog's collar made of iron. It was riveted together so that they couldn't take it off.

Godred Crovan starts Tynwald
1079

Battle of Santwat
1098

Andreas, for example, is named after the man who set it up. Thorwald had his name carved in runes along the side. Runes are the Viking way of writing and these say: 'Thorwald raised the cross…' Lots of the Manx crosses show pictures of the long stories called sagas which the Vikings loved. The Thorwald cross shows the god Týr with the raven of Óðin on his shoulder, tying up the wolf Fenrir. Fashions change and today we wouldn't put non-Christian stories like Týr and Fenrir onto a Christian symbol like a cross. Vikings didn't worry about that though. They believed in lots of different gods. To Vikings the Christian God was just one more and they added him to their list of gods quite soon after they moved to Mann.

DID YOU KNOW?

The coast of Norway, if straightened out, is long enough to go round the Earth 2½ times.

Introducing Tynwald

Like most invaders, the Vikings who came to live in the Isle of Man brought their own way of doing things. As they were now in charge they made sure that everyone else did things the way the Vikings wanted them done. Most of the Vikings who moved to the Isle of Man came from Norway, where people lived in small groups. Norway has a very frilly coast with lots of sea inlets, while the land consists mainly of mountains and rivers. Getting from place to place was difficult so the different groups of people didn't meet up very often. To make sure that they didn't start fighting when they did get together – these are Vikings remember, who loved quarrelling – the men organised formal meetings from time to time to make up rules which people had to live by. These formal rule-making meetings were called *þings* or *things* – the letter *þ* sounds like a *th*. The Vikings didn't have a building big enough to get everyone in, so

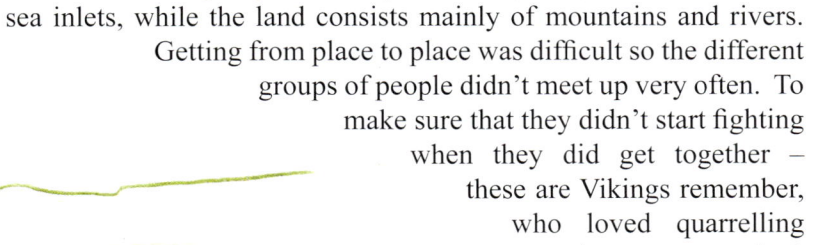

Monks start building Rushen Abbey
1134

þings were held outside on a special field called a *völlr*. The open-air meetings were therefore called *þing-völlr* and that's where Tynwald gets its name. Vikings brought Tynwald to the Isle of Man and it's been meeting ever since. It's the oldest continuous parliament in the world.

Vikings would probably recognise a lot of what happens on Tynwald Day today, except that they wouldn't have allowed girls to take part. Vikings held their *things* on a small hill, like Tynwald Hill, so people watching could see what was going on. They also added to the hill a handful of earth which each group had brought with them from home. This meant that all the people meeting would think of themselves as being on homeground. Vikings were very polite to visitors, so the handfuls of earth helped them to stop quarrelling. Tynwald Hill is also said to be made of earth from every parish in the island.

When Vikings chose their *þing-völlr* they made a holy or sacred area to the east of the meeting hill – just like St John's Church is east of Tynwald Hill. The holy area was where judges decided what to do with people who had broken the rules.

Tynwald Day is 5 July. Midsummer was a good time for Vikings to meet as there was plenty of light to make travelling easier, the weather wouldn't be cold, and it was also the time of the Viking festival celebrating the longest day. An excellent reason for a party!

But who was in charge?

We've all heard of dukes and earls, well the Viking top people were called *jarls*. They were rich and had lots of supporters which they used as a private army if they needed to. The jarls' job was to ensure that their followers stayed rich and safe, and jarls could be sacked or killed if they weren't good at leading or fighting. Their supporters were called *karls* and were farmers, boatbuilders and smiths. Just as today ordinary people can become Members of the House of Keys if they get enough votes, so karls could become jarls if they showed enough skill and daring in a fight. Women were not allowed to be leaders officially, but usually

Reginald I reigns for one day

1164

managed to influence the men. Below the karls were *þræll* or thralls who were servants, and below the thralls were slaves.

Godred Crovan was a Manx karl with ambition. He wanted to be a jarl. Even more than that, he wanted to rule the Isle of Man. He didn't grow up on the island but came back in 1079 with an army of three hundred men. They rowed up the Sulby River from Ramsey until they got to just beyond Milntown. Then they hid their boats, walked to Sky Hill and hid in the trees on the slopes – the Lezayre Road wasn't there then of course. The local army came to kick Godred and his men out but were sandwiched between the hill and the river and didn't have the room to fight properly, so Godred won. In Manx, Godred is Goree so Godred Crovan is better known as King Goree or King Orry.

Once in charge Godred decided how the Isle of Man should be run – and it still runs like that today. He also, as a good jarl should, rewarded his followers, i.e. his army, for their help. This meant giving them land for farming or a lot of captured booty if they wanted to go back home – Godred hadn't been living on Mann, remember, so a lot of his men were not Manx.

Godred might have been born on the island, but local people didn't like being chased off their farms by his followers who were, after all, only come-overs. Twenty years later the Manx rebelled. People still argue over who actually won the Battle of Santwat in 1098, but it doesn't really matter. Both sides fought until they were tired. Then King Magnus III of Norway sailed in and took over the island. Neither Godred, nor the Manx had enough energy left to stop him.

Naughty names?

The new king's nickname was Magnus *Barfot*, which means Magnus Barelegs. It sounds a bit chilly. He was a Viking and so wore the normal Viking clothes of a long tunic with a belt, but he didn't like wearing the

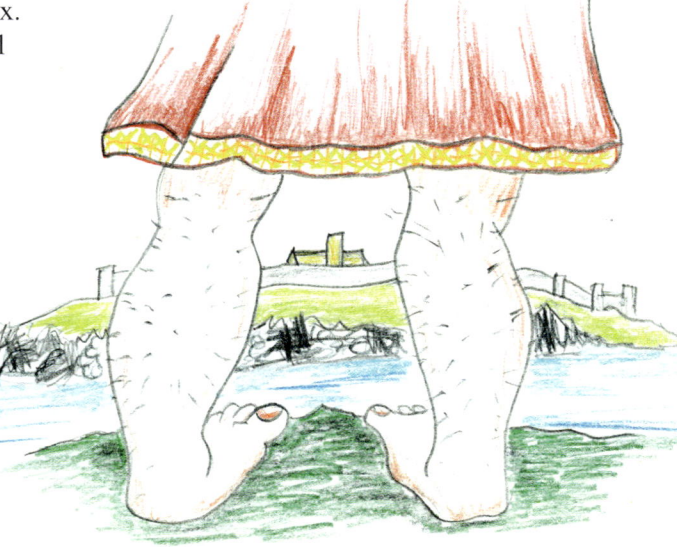

> **DID YOU KNOW?**
>
> Piles of rocks were used as signposts. They marked the best route to get to the things and also marked fords, etc.

17

trousers which normally went underneath the tunic, so he didn't wear them. He was a king who loved fighting and was very good at it so people didn't criticise his fashion sense. Not if they wanted to stay alive.

It was probably Magnus Barelegs who started building the castle on St Patrick's Isle just off Peel. King Magnus had already taken over parts of Scotland and so had got a bit big headed thinking that no-one could stop him from taking whatever he wanted. After capturing Mann he decided he wanted Ireland too and invaded. He didn't get it though; he was killed.

Olaf I, who was the son of King Orry, took over the Isle of Man in 1103. His nickname was 'The Dwarf' but there was nothing small about his ability; he ruled Mann for the next fifty years.

King Magnus built a castle, but King Olaf founded an abbey and gave some land at Rushen to the abbot of Furness. If you draw a straight line east (that's to the right) from Rushen Abbey, Furness is the chunk of land in the UK your pencil would get to first. Furness Abbey is inland but very close to your line. The monks from Furness started building Rushen Abbey in 1134. It took them a long time, and they would have started building in wood to make sure they had somewhere to live. Then they would have gradually replaced the wooden buildings with stone ones.

As well as being places where people could pray and study, abbey rules said that the abbey must grow its own food, offer somewhere for travellers to stay, care for the sick and look after the poor. Abbeys were therefore a mix of school, farm, hospital, charity and bed & breakfast. Doing all this needed a lot of people so abbeys also became landlords, with some of their land rented out to local farmers. Rushen Abbey eventually came to own land near Sulby, Peel, Port St Mary and Port Erin.

Squabbles

You only need to look at the news today to realise that followers of a religion aren't necessarily peaceful people. It was just the same with some of the Christians on the Isle of Man. The Christian church is ruled by bishops.

DID YOU KNOW?

The Hebrides were known as the Southern Islands or *Suðoer* (pronounced, roughly, 'soo-ther'), while Orkney and Shetland were the Northern Islands or *Norðoer* ('nor-ther'). Because of the way it looks when written down, *Suðoer* soon came to be pronounced Soder, so the bishop in charge of the church in the Isle of Man was called the Bishop of Sodor and Man. He still is.

Building starts on St German's Cathedral
1230

Today a bishop is only appointed after lots of discussions and committees have decided that they're the right person. In mediaeval times bishops were given the job on the say-so of a particular person. The bishop-making person was always important and often an archbishop. He could gave people the job of bishop merely because he wanted to pay back a debt or reward one of his gang. It's rather like a football manager giving someone the job of goalkeeper because they'd bought the team a minibus.

At this time the Isle of Man was part of a larger kingdom ruled by Vikings and made up of lots of other island including the Hebrides (to the west of Scotland) and Shetland and Orkney (to the north of Scotland). Olaf, as the ruler of Mann, thought he had the right to decide who should be bishop. The abbot of Furness Abbey, as the owner of the biggest Christian church on the island, also thought he should have a say. Then there was the Archbishop of Nidaros (now called Trondheim) in Norway who thought he should decide, as the King of Norway was boss-king of King Olaf. Finally there was the Archbishop of York, who seems to have thought that he could appoint the bishop, as he was in charge of the churches in the north of England. It was all terribly confusing and often meant that there was more than one Bishop of Sodor and Man appointed by different people. Bishop Simon, bishop 1226-1247, was the first man to be accepted by everyone. Whoever had the job had somewhere nice to live though. Bishopscourt.

If the confusion in the church wasn't enough, there was also a lot of confusion about who ruled the island. For the next two hundred years the kings of Norway, Ireland and then Scotland and England argued and fought over who should rule Mann. Sometimes kings lasted a few years, sometimes only a few days. Occasionally defeated kings came back to power. King Reginald I grabbed the throne but only sat on it for four days before being kicked off by his brother. Reginald seems to have been an unlucky name as eighty or so years later another King Reginald didn't last much longer. He ruled for twenty-fours days before being defeated in battle.

Eventually Magnus IV, the last Manx King, died, and the island was ruled by the King of Norway. He had his own country to worry about and so, in 1266, sold the Isle of Man to Alexander III, King of Scotland. Manx independence was over.

Reginald II reigns for one day
1249

Magnus sells Mann to Alexander
1266

CHAPTER 3

MEDIAEVAL MANN

A new ruler meant new rules. To start with, the new king wanted people to know he was in charge. Today you recognise your favourite sweets or shoes or football team by their brand, label or badge. It was no different eight hundred years ago. The Vikings used a picture of one of their longships as their badge. The new team was Scottish and didn't want any Norwegian reminders, thank you very much. Alexander – he was the Scottish king and therefore captain of the top team – introduced a three-legged symbol and the island has been known by the Three Legs of Man ever since.

The Manx fight the Scots

Not that the Scots ruled for very long. The Manx didn't like their new bosses. They didn't like the way these strangers treated the islanders as second class. They didn't like the way the come-overs didn't fit in with the island way of doing things. And they definitely didn't like all the new taxes they suddenly had to pay.

The Manx grumbled for about ten years – *traa dy liooar* – then they decided to do something about it. In 1275 Godred, son of Magnus IV, the last King of Mann, led a Manx rebellion. Unfortunately it didn't work. Alexander III landed troops at Ronaldsway and Godred was killed in the battle. The Scots were still in charge.

In fact they stayed in charge for another eleven years, until Alexander III died, in 1286. His throne was inherited by his granddaughter Margaret. She was known as 'the Maid of Norway' as her father was king of Norway. She was only three. Other leaders didn't like the idea of being ruled by a foreign child – and a girl at that. Not macho enough. They also thought that a crown would probably look very nice on them, so fighting started all over again.

DID YOU KNOW?

There is no rule which says which way the Three Legs of Man should be running.

The Main Mann!

The kings on all the surrounding islands – Scotland, Ireland, England, Wales – all wanted to own the Isle of Man because of where it was. The sea was very, very important for travelling.

Godred leads unsuccessful Manx rebellion · Alexander III dies

1275 · 1286

> **DID YOU KNOW?**
>
> The sea was sometimes called the 'sail road' or 'whale way'

Today people travel mostly by road or air, and things to be sold (often called 'trading goods') are also carried around by road or air. Eight hundred years ago there were no roads and certainly no aeroplanes. People either walked or, if they were rich enough, rode a horse, or they went by boat. To get goods to places which were not on the coast, traders would either carry them in packs on their back, or use pack ponies. Some of the roads the pack carriers used still exist; the footpath coming down from Ballaragh to Laxey harbour is one such. The old pack horse route is called Puncheon Road or Laxey Old Road and was once the only path into the old village of Laxey.

Eight hundred years ago no vehicles on the Isle of Man had wheels, so you can forget horse-drawn waggons   Anything too big to be carried by people or ponies would probably have been put on a sledge which ran on grass. They were called carrs.

The difficulty of getting things inland was why most people – not everyone, but most people – lived by the coast, or at least near a river. If a village or farm was by water, it could be reached by boat. Even if someone went from Peel to Castletown, for example, the chances are that they'd have gone by boat. People travelled by sea, they traded by sea, they went visiting by sea, they got in touch with distant friends and relatives by sea. The sea was crowded with small boats bustling round the coastline between ports, or butting across the Irish Sea, collecting and delivering cargoes and passengers and parcels and letters. In mediaeval times the sea was like a cross between an airport and the internet.

The Isle of Man was in the middle of the sea and so was in the middle of all this activity. It was an excellent place for boats to stop if they were going from England to Ireland, or Scotland to Wales – or the other way round. Mann provided shelter from storms. It was also a good place to be if you wanted to attack or control the ships. Kings noticed.

Edward I of England claims the Isle of Man
1290

Squabbles and supporters

The toughest king in the area was Edward I of England. Edward had the biggest army, the fiercest temper and the most battle experience, so of course he was always right. When he said that the Isle of Man had always belonged to him no-one was going to argue. He and his son Edward II ruled the island for about twenty years, although they never visited it. Then trouble started again. By now the Scots had a new king, Robert the Bruce, and he wanted the island back.

Over the next twelve years or so, the English and Scots squabbled over the island with sometimes Edward II of England ruling and sometimes Robert I ('The Bruce') of Scotland. Things didn't settle down until yet another king, Edward III of England, decided that enough was enough. He ordered his army to invade Mann and the island has been ruled from England ever since.

> Edward I was called Edward Longshanks because he was very tall. Historians also call him The Hammer of the Scots, because he kept interfering in Scottish rule, often at sword point. He was never called The Hammer of the Scots at the time.
>
> Robert the Bruce got his name from his family name which was 'de Brus' or 'de Bruis'. If you say 'de Brus' it sounds like 'the Bruce', which is what it became. Two hundred years before, the de Brus family were come-overs from France and their name meant 'from Brus'. The village is in Normandy and is now called Brix.

And what did the Manx want? Well, nobody thought to ask them, but they did the best they could, trying not to upset whoever happened to be on island at the time and trying to earn a living from either side in turn. The problem was that farms often weren't big enough to produce enough food to support a large family. Sometimes whichever leader was fighting at the time would also take the farm's food, which meant the Manx went even hungrier. To earn extra, men went fishing or mining, while women ran the farm.

The quiet power

Apart from the rulers and the ruled – kings and ordinary people – there was a third group of people who lived on Mann and had a lot of influence in farming, trading and how things were done. The church. Seven hundred years ago bishops and abbots had a lot more power than they do now.

Rushen Abbey belonged to a group of monks called Cistercians, whose regional headquarters was Furness Abbey across the water in England. Rushen Abbey owned almost half the land in Malew parish, as well as large chunks of German and Lezayre, and smaller parcels of land in Rushen, Lonan and Maughold. Cistercians were expert sheep farmers and, as everyone wore woollen clothing, the monks got very rich. In fact they became so rich that Furness Abbey had its own fleet of trading ships.

Imposition of the smoke penny   Robert the Bruce takes over
1302   1313

Seven hundred years ago the king allowed anyone who owned a lot of land to call himself a Baron. The church owned a lot of land so the Bishop of Sodor and Man became a Bishop Baron, and the church land became known as barony land.

Barons were allowed to run their own courts and to punish people who broke the law. The Abbot of Rushen Abbey and the Bishop of Sodor and Man each had a barony court. Most punishments involved paying a fine, but some crimes were punished by death. The abbot's gallows were on Black Hill, north east of the abbey. The Monks' Bridge at Ballasalla was new in 1350, and not only made it easier to get to the abbey land on the other side of the Silverburn River, it also made it easier for spectators to get to the abbot's gallows.

After a while the church got a bit above itself. The secular (non-church) leaders tended to be more interested in running the Isle of Man, so Church leaders began to see themselves as far more important than they really were and passed a lot of laws when the kings weren't looking. The church also taxed people – not just those living on lands the church owned, but everyone. People had to pay tithes, or one tenth of everything they earned. Let's say you get £5.00 pocket money per week. You'd have to give 50p of that to the church.

One tax which nobody liked was imposed by Bishop Mark. He insisted that every house with a fireplace should pay the church one penny per year. It doesn't sound like a lot, but it was about the same as two week's pay today. The tax was called the 'smoke penny'. It was deeply unpopular as everyone used their fire for warmth and cooking.

> **DID YOU KNOW?**
>
> The hill between Dhoon Glen and Ballaglass Glen on the north east coast is still called the Barony and used to belong to Rushen Abbey.

> **DID YOU KNOW?**
>
> The smoke penny tax was paid for over five hundred years.

Edward III of England becomes King of Mann — 1329

William Montacute King of Mann under Edward — 1334

Lots of learning

The church was also in charge of education, although pupils weren't taught the same sorts of things as they learn today. In fact girls didn't go to school at all, but were taught sewing and cooking by their mothers at home. Most boys were taught a trade by their fathers – usually farming and fishing. A few boys were taught by monks, either so that they could become monks themselves, or because they had rich fathers who wanted their sons to take over the family estate. Monks would teach boys to read, write and do sums, so they would be able to keep their own records.

The Isle of Man, of course, has its own language, but the monks wouldn't teach Manx children in Manx. They'd use Latin, the language of the church. At least they would if they spoke it themselves. All the fighting between Scotland and England messed everything up including the training of new monks and priests. Because of this quite a lot of the clergy didn't know Latin, so couldn't teach it to their pupils.

Manx for the many

The clergy had a lot of say in how the Isle of Man was run and made it a rule that everyone went to church. Church services were held in Latin; even if the priest didn't understand much Latin, he learnt the words of the service off by heart. Bishop William thought it was wrong that ordinary people couldn't understand what was going on in church. He told his priests to teach people the apostles' creed in Manx.

> **The first line of the apostles creed**
>
> In English: 'I believe in God the Father Almighty, Maker of heaven and earth...'
> In Latin: 'Credo in Deum Patrem Omnipotentem, Creatorem caeli et terrae...'
> In Manx: 'Ta mee credjal ayns Jee yn Ayr Ooilley-niartal, Chroo niau as thalloo...'

In fact the Manx could probably speak bits of a lot of different languages, because the fishing and trading ships visited all the countries round the island, and often went to Europe and Scandinavia too. Manx sailors, like sailors everywhere, picked up words and phrases from other countries. The languages of Scotland, Ireland and Wales are very similar to Manx, so talking with visitors from those countries wouldn't have been a problem. Up to around 1362 the official language of England was… French! (William the

Rebuild of Castle Rushen starts
1340

Apostles Creed in Manx
1350

Conqueror had taken over England in 1066 and he was from Normandy which is part of France. As he won he got to make the rules.) English was spoken in England of course, but only by people who weren't considered very important – those doing the work rather than making the decisions. The arrangement of French/English in England during the fourteenth century was like the arrangement of English/Manx today on the Isle of Man. In England in the fourteenth century the official stuff was done in French, although everyone spoke English; today on the Isle of Man most of the official stuff is done in English, but Manx is the real language.

Kings and things

OK, so Edward III of England now 'owned' the Isle of Man. He didn't want to bother with running it though, as he was too busy fighting Scotland and quarrelling with France. One of the king's best friends was William Montagu (or Montacute, or even de Monte Acuto – spelling was more flexible then) so Edward decided that William could rule Mann. Not that the island's new ruler came here very often as King Edward kept him too busy.

One thing William did find time for though was repairing Castle Rushen as Robert the Bruce had damaged it rather badly when he was in charge. In fact so many repairs were needed that William Montecute, or rather his Manx builders, built most of what is left today.

> **DID YOU KNOW?**
>
> A century which lasts, for example, from 1300 to 1399 is called the fourteenth century because the years 1 to 99 weren't called the 'zero-th' century (that would be silly!), but the first century. Years 100 to 199 then had to be the second century, 200 to 299 the third century and so on.
>
> An easy way to remember is to add one on if you're using numbers, e.g. 1100s (plus 1) becomes twelfth century, or take one off if you're using words, e.g. fourteenth century (minus 1) becomes 1300s.

William's son, another William, took over in 1344 after his father died. Like his father, he spent most of his time fighting the Scots and French on behalf of the King of England. He didn't care much about Mann either, but when he did visit he lived in Castle Rushen, the house his Dad had built. This caused a bit of a problem as the capital city was wherever the king lived. Before William, the King of Mann had lived in Peel Castle. Moving to Castle Rushen meant that the capital city moved too. Castletown began to be more important than Peel.

William was also in charge of the Isle of Wight, off the south coast of England, and was Admiral of the English fleet. He lived mainly at Bisham Abbey in Berkshire, not far from London, and obviously thought

Richard II becomes King of England — 1377

Mann sold to Richard Le Scrope for son William, friend of Richard II — 1393

that the Isle of Man was too far from the action. Having a spare island, he sold Mann to Richard le Scrope for £10,000. Richard wanted the island for his son, yet another William. He got the island cheap!

> **DID YOU KNOW?**
>
> £10,000 in the fourteenth century would be about £230 million today.

Meanwhile there had been a change of English king. Edward III died in 1377 and Richard II took over the throne. He and Richard le Scrope's son William were great friends. This turned out to be a pity. Richard II reigned for twenty-two years, but wasn't a good king and was eventually kicked out by Henry IV. To make it clear who was now in charge Henry also beheaded Richard's loyal servant William le Scrope.

William's death meant that the crown of Mann lacked a head to wear it. King Henry gave the island to Henry Percy, but five years later Percy and a lot of his neighbours in the north of England, including the Archibishop of York, decided that they'd prefer to be in charge of a lot more. King Henry wasn't having that and, having defeated the rebels, gave the Isle of Man to Sir John Stanley, one of the people who had fought on his side.

Henry IV probably saw the gift as a reward for Sir John's loyalty. He didn't realise that Sir John's family would rule the Isle of Man for the next 350 years.

Richard II ousted, William le Scrope beheaded
New King Henry IV gives the Isle of Man to Henry Percy

Henry IV gives Isle of Man to Sir John Stanley

1399

1405

CHAPTER 4

KING... STANLEY?

So, Sir John Stanley became King of Man. King Henry IV of England, who'd given the island to Sir John, said that the Stanleys could only keep the kingship if they gave two falcons to every new king or queen of England on the day they were crowned. He wanted to make sure that the Stanley family remembered that they were only in charge because the English king said so.

The new rulers take charge

Sir John Stanley doesn't seem to have been very impressed with his new kingdom as he didn't come here. His son did though. He was also called John and visited several times. He also took the top spot at a couple of meetings of Tynwald.

The organisation of Tynwald is almost exactly the same today as it was in Sir John's time. The king or lord sits on top of Tynwald Hill with all the officials on the different levels below. During the procession the sword of state is carried upright in front of the King or Lord of Mann. The sword carried today is probably the same sword which was carried in front of Sir John Stanley six hundred years ago. At least the hilt is. The blade was probably replaced about five hundred years ago.

One of the Stanley falcons appears on the left of the Manx coat of arms today. A raven stands on the right because Odin had two ravens as companions and the raven is a reminder of the island's Viking past. The falcon and the raven are called supporters and hold the Three Legs of Man on a shield between them.

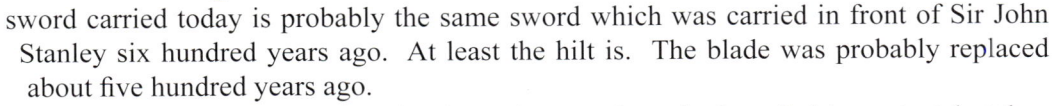

People wanted to rule the Isle of Man because it made them feel important, but they also had other jobs – usually being the ruler of somewhere else – and mostly left the island to run itself. Because of this the church had taken over a lot of things like laws and punishments. The second Sir John decided that this had to change.

He began to write down the laws. It sounds obvious, but it made things much fairer as the same punishments could then be handed out for the same crimes. Before that people had to rely on their memories, and punishments could be what the judge felt like at the time. The church had also been able to interfere with the law by protecting criminals; Sir John stopped that too.

The first Manx laws are written down

1422

As we saw in chapter 3, the church had become rich partly because it owned a lot of land and partly because it made everyone pay the church a tithe or tenth of their income. Most people didn't have the sort of job which paid them in money, so farmers paid their tithes in crops or cattle, millers in bags of flour, fishermen in fish and so on. A lot of the tithe income went off island to the church's headquarters in England. Sir John couldn't stop the tithes but could and did stop the church exporting Manx wealth.

Sir John also insisted on knowing who visited the church leaders. He probably remembered the rebellion which made his dad King of Man. One member of the losing side was the Archbishop of York, remember.

> **DID YOU KNOW?**
>
> Ever heard of 'roll call'? That's asking people to say whether they are here, so that it can be recorded. A roll is an old name for a record. It's called a roll because records and laws used to be written on rolls of paper.

The Keys of the kingdom

The House of Keys is the name of part of the Manx parliament. If you see someone with MHK written after their name, it means that they are a Member of the House of Keys, and therefore a member of the Manx parliament. In the Manx parliament a Key is a person and not something you undo a lock with.

The number of Keys hasn't changed for hundreds of years. There are twenty four today and, in Sir John's time, in the early fourteenth century, there were also twenty four. In fact there has been the same number of Keys for such a long time that the MHKs are often called 'The Twenty Four'.

We don't know exactly who decided on the number or when it was decided, but we do know where the name comes from. Probably. A famous Manx historian, who was also Speaker (i.e. leader) of the House of Keys – he was called A.W. Moore – thought that 'Keys' probably came from some clumsy English clerk trying to pronounce the first part of *kiare-as-feed*, which is Manx for 'twenty four'. The clerk got it wrong, wrote it down wrongly, and accidentally invented the term Keys.

Wherever the name came from, the twenty-four men – sorry girls, six hundred years ago the Keys would have had to be men – had to be over twenty one and own Manx land. People like fishermen, merchants, miners or workers like blacksmiths, who did not own land were not allowed to be Keys. It didn't matter how rich you were, if you didn't own land then you couldn't be one of the Twenty Four. This caused problems later!

The Keys were there to tell the ruler what the people wanted – not that he often took much notice. Unlike today the Keys weren't paid for their work, but they didn't have to do some things which everyone else had to.

Look out!

One of the main jobs everyone had to do – or at least all the men (except those who were very young, very old, or had jobs like being Keys) – was Watch and Ward. 'Watch' meant exactly what it does today, while 'Ward' meant defending somewhere. To protect the island, men took it in turns to keep watch from hills around the coast. If they saw enemy boats they raised the alarm. This gave their families time to collect their valuables and hide. Meanwhile their neighbours would be gathering together to fight off invaders.

Watch and Ward was invented by the Vikings and carried on until after the Second World War. Different hills were used for the day watch and the night watch. Those used during the day were called *cronk ny arrey laa* (hill of the day watch), the hills used at night, *cronk ny arrey oie* (hill of the night watch). The names of many look-out hills are still the same today, although the spelling might have changed a bit.

Look-out hills

Cronk ny Arrey Laa, near Poyllvaaish, Arbory
Cronk ny Arrey Laa, at Shellag Point, Bride
Cronk ny Arrey Lhaa, near Jurby Church, Jurby
Cronk ny Irey Lhaa, near Lonan Old Church, Lonan
Cronk y Watch, near Knockaloe, Patrick
Cronk ny Arrey, near Cregneash, Rushen
Cronk ny Arrey Laa, south of Eairy Cushlin, Rushen
    (Eairy Cushlin is in Patrick, but Cronk ny Arrey Laa is just over the border in Rushen)

There were others of course – Slieau Lewaigue was used as a day-time look-out in Maughold, for example – but they're often called something else.

How did people live?

So what was life like for ordinary people? Hard work! Women were much better treated on the Isle of Man than they would have been in England, though. They

Thomas Stanley sorts out local riots

1507

could own their own property and have a say in what happened to them. English women couldn't.

Most ordinary people worked at farming, fishing and mining, often doing a little of each. Their animals lived in the same house as the people, partly to keep them safe and partly to provide warmth.

Food was much more boring than it is today as people ate the same things almost all the time. Herring and oat cakes were the main food, with water, milk or buttermilk to drink. Once potatoes had been discovered and brought back from America, the Manx had those too. Farm animals were kept for milk and/or wool, so people didn't eat meat very often. People collected fruit from the hedgerows and also eggs from seabirds. They ate the birds too, if they could catch them.

> **DID YOU KNOW?**
>
> A traditional Manx blessing is *palchey puddase as skeddan dy liooar* (potatoes in plenty and herring enough).

Left to get on with it!

Back to those in charge. The second Sir John Stanley might have been interested in the island, but his son and grandson weren't and didn't come here. In fact it took seventy years for the island's ruler to visit it again.

Thomas Stanley – he wasn't called 'sir' any more, as his grandfather had been promoted to being the Earl of Derby. Just to confuse everyone, if you're talking to the Earl of Derby you should call him Lord Derby. In fact Thomas Stanley was also King of Mann, but preferred being called Lord of Mann. King Henry VII of England was Thomas's overlord and very jealous of anyone else claiming to be a king. As Henry had a habit of killing people he didn't like, Thomas thought that being called Lord of Mann (and not King) would be safer.

Rushen Abbey closed by Henry VIII of England

1540

His full title made Thomas Stanley sound like a crowd. He was Lord of Mann, 2nd Earl of Derby, Baron Stanley, Baron Strange and Baron Mohun, but only the first two really counted and the rest were often left out. He visited the island in 1507 to stop some riots, and they did stop – it's always difficult to refuse the boss. The bay where he landed was named Derbyhaven in his honour, and still is.

The First Manx Book

The Stanley family, i.e. the Earls of Derby, were still in charge a hundred years after the christening of Derbyhaven, when the first book written in Manx was published. As clergymen were the people who could read and write best, it's not surprising that the writer of the first book in Manx was a bishop. What is surprising is that he wasn't Manx!

Bishop John Phillips came from North Wales and became Bishop of Sodor and Man in 1604. As well as English he spoke Welsh, and Welsh is very similar to Manx, so he had a headstart in learning the island's language. Not only did he want the people under his care to understand him, he wanted them to understand what went on in church. The problem was that the prayer book was in English. Bishop John decided to translate it.

He did have help from his nextdoor neighbour. The Rev Hugh Cannell was the Vicar of Kirk Michael, next door to Bishopscourt where the bishop lived. Rev Hugh was also a Manxman who spoke Manx so was a good person to help his boss.

It was 1610 when Bishop John and Rev Hugh finished their translation, so it took them several years. Even then it wasn't printed. Lots of people couldn't afford printed books so, if they wanted their own copy, they did just that – copied it. By hand.

Stanley, the come-over

The rulers of the Isle of Man had a habit of not coming here, but that changed with the 7th Earl. James Stanley, 7th Earl of Derby, not only visited far more than any other member of his family, he even lived here for a few years.

The Manx called James *Y Stanlagh Moare*, which means The Great Stanley. He ruled the island for nearly twenty-five years and a lot happened. One of the first things James did was to start racing horses on Langness, where the golf course is now. His excuse was that he wanted to improve the Manx horses, but what he really wanted was to have fun. Charles I of England liked horse racing. James Stanley liked the king. He wanted to follow the new fashion.

DID YOU KNOW?

All languages change over the years and spelling also changes, but Bishop John and Rev Hugh's prayer book in Manx is still very similar to the Manx one used today.

Publication of first book written in Manx — 1610

The first Manx Derby — 1627

STANLEY FAMILY TREE

Sir John Stanley (1350-1414), King of Mann (1405-1414)

Sir John Stanley (1386-1437), King of Mann (1414-1437)

Sir Thomas Stanley (1405-1459), King of Mann (1437-1459), 1st Baron Stanley

Thomas Stanley (1435-1504), King of Mann (1459-1504), 1st Earl of Derby

    George Stanley (1460-1503), Lord Strange

Thomas Stanley (1485-1521), Lord of Mann (1504-1521), 2nd Earl of Derby

Edward Stanley (1509-1572), Lord of Mann (1521-1572), 3rd Earl of Derby

Henry Stanley (1531-1593), Lord of Mann (1572-1593), 4th Earl of Derby

Ferdinando Stanley (1559-1594)	William Stanley (1561-1642)	*married to*	Elizabeth de Vere (1575-1627)
Lord of Mann (1593-1594)	Lord of Mann (1609-1612)		Lord of Mann (1612-1627)
5th Earl of Derby	(succession disputed, hence the delay)		Countess of Derby
	5th Earl of Derby		

James Stanley (1607-1651)
Lord of Mann (1627-1651)
7th Earl of Derby

English Civil War
Thomas Fairfax (1612-1671)
Lord of Mann (1651-1660)
3rd Lord Fairfax of Cameron

Charles Stanley (1628-1672)
Lord of Mann (1660-1672)
8th Earl of Derby

William Stanley (1655-1702)	James Stanley (1664-1736)
Lord of Mann (1672-1702)	Lord of Mann (1702-1736)
9th Earl of Derby	10th Earl of Derby

James Stanley's sons died before he did, so the Lordship of Mann went to a distant cousin, James Murray, 2nd Duke of Atholl. He was the great grandson of the 7th Earl of Derby and the grandson of the 7th Earl's daughter, Amelia who married John Murray, 1st Marquess of Atholl.

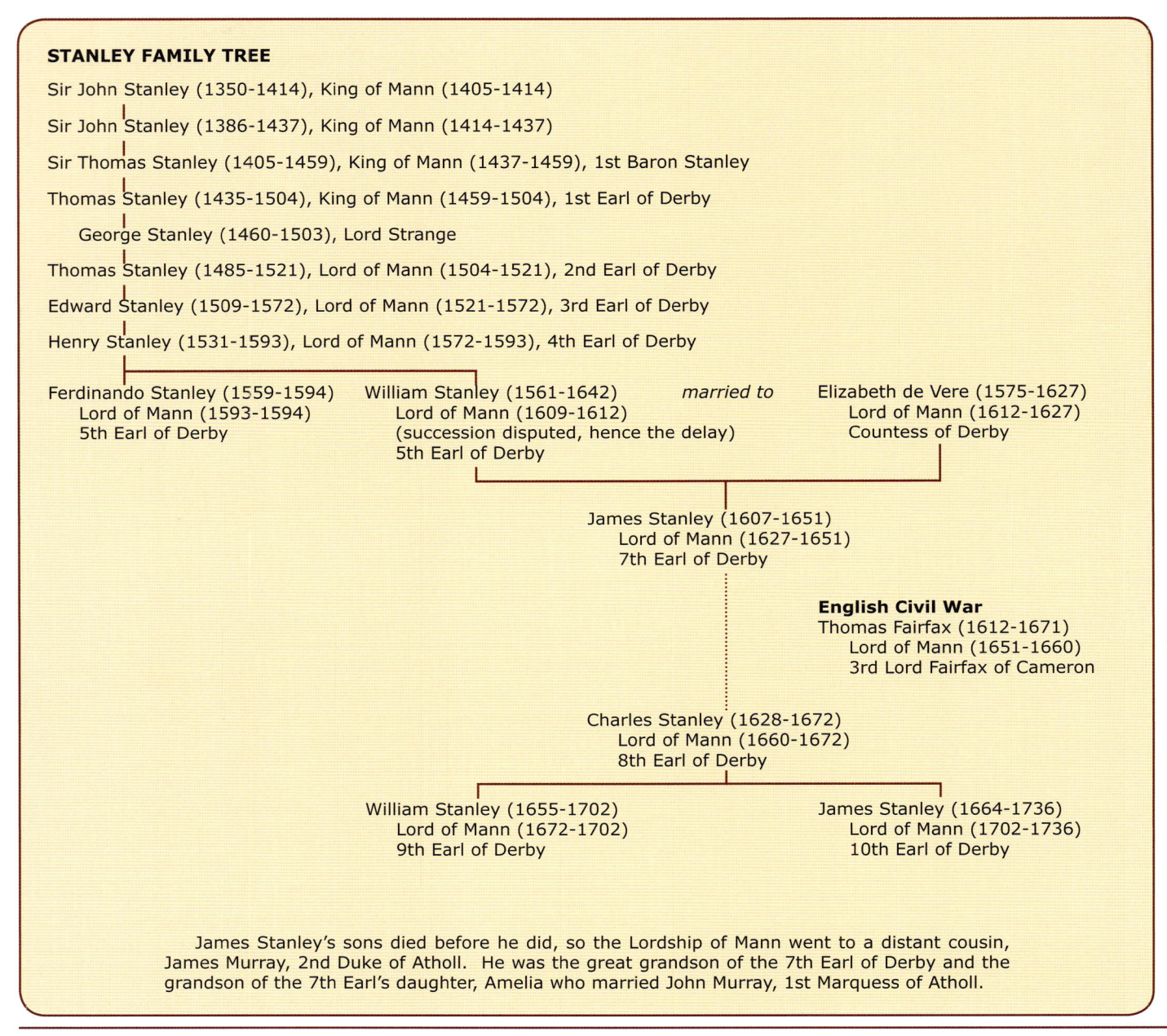

Start of English Civil War

1642

The Great Stanley's liking for the king caused him quite a lot of problems. A war had just started in England between people who preferred being ruled by parliament and those who preferred being ruled by the king. James Stanley obviously supported the king. Because he did, the Isle of Man had to.

While James Stanley was in England fighting for King Charles, he'd left Manxman Edward Christian in charge of the island. Edward was tough. He'd been a privateer – which is a posh word for a pirate, although one acting inside rather than outside the law. Manx law said that Edward was an honest seafaring merchant. English law said that he was a smuggler. He trained James's private army and was in charge of making sure no-one caused any trouble.

It was a bit serious, then, when James found out that Edward had been telling people not to pay their tithes. Tithes were a tenth of everything you owned which you had to pay to the church, remember. Edward lost his job and went to prison.

The war between the king and parliament was still going on in England and The Great Stanley wanted to make sure that the English parliament didn't get their hands on the Isle of Man. He and his troops kept Watch and Ward (remember that?), and built forts to defend the island.

James even had a few ships kitted out to fight. It wasn't all to help the English king. The Stanley family needed somewhere safe to live. In 1644 they moved into Castle Rushen.

Now, it had always been the job of the Manx to make sure that the people in Castle Rushen had enough to eat and drink. That meant not only The Great Stanley

James Stanley and his family move to Mann

1644

and his family, but also all his servants and soldiers (and their families and visitors and hangers-on…). That might have been bad enough, but James said that anyone fighting for King Charles would also be welcome and safe in Castle Rushen. The king was losing the war – in fact he lost so badly he lost his head – so Castle Rushen had a lot of people living in it. The Manx were expected to feed them all. Without being paid!

Not surprisingly, the local people got a bit annoyed at having to provide all this free food and wood for the fires and so on. They didn't really care who was in charge in a different country, but did care about what happened to them in theirs. James had also tried to change the rules about owning Manx land, and the Manx farmers definitely didn't like that. They were getting ready to rebel when James took some soldiers to England to help on the king's side. He never came back. The king's team lost so badly that James was caught. Like the king, he had his head cut off.

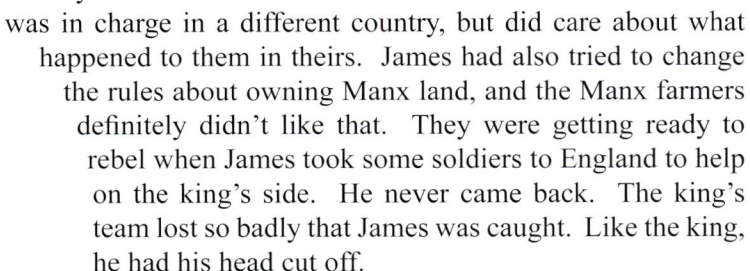

DID YOU KNOW?

There's the base of a Civil War fort at Ballachurry. It's called Kerroogarroo Fort and was built to defend the northern end of the island in case parliamentary troops – that's the English parliament and not the Manx one – invaded.

James Stanley, 7th Earl of Derby was beheaded on 15 October 1651 in Bolton, England. He is buried in Ormskirk, near the west coast of England.

The man wielding the axe was George Whewell. He isn't buried anywhere, or rather not all of him is. His skull rests behind the bar of the Pack Horse Inn, Affetside, near Bury (appropriate!), England. He gets very cross if anyone moves it. Those who have tried report being threatened by a ghostly headsman waving an axe…

Charles I of England beheaded
1649

James Stanley 'The Great Stanley' beheaded
Castle Rushen surrenders
1651

34

CHAPTER 5

MAKING MONEY AND MISCHIEF

To recap; in 1651 the Earl of Derby and Lord of Mann was dead. His widow was holding the fort, the fort in this case being Castle Rushen. The British king was also dead. The UK parliament was running Britain and calling it a Commonwealth. The king's son and the earl's son – both called Charles – were running in France, but they were on the run. Who was running the Isle of Man?

Not King – Commonwealth…

Countess Charlotte, the earl's widow, thought she was in charge, but the Manx had other ideas. William Christian was a farmer in Ronaldsway, and also in charge of the militia – the earl's private Manx army. He was better known as Illiam Dhone, Brown William.

Illiam Dhone didn't like the old earl's ideas about owning land, and definitely didn't like his island being used as a football between the old rulers and the new one. He decided to do something about it. Charlotte barricaded her family inside Castle Rushen and had troops defending Peel Castle, but Illiam was soon in charge of the rest of the island.

Neither Countess Charlotte, nor Illiam Dhone thought that the Isle of Man could be independent of the Commonwealth. The Commonwealth armies were too good. At the same time they hoped to get a good deal, and definitely didn't want to be invaded. Charlotte wanted to swop the island for her husband (she didn't know he was dead), while Illiam wanted to make sure that any ruler of the island obeyed the Manx laws. Colonel Robert Duckenfield, in charge of parliamentary troops, was already anchored in Ramsey Bay and getting ready to invade. As Illiam Dhone was running most of the Isle of Man, the people running the Commonwealth talked with Illiam, not Charlotte.

Illiam and his Manx troops allowed Robert and his Commonwealth troops to land. Robert then told Charlotte that her husband was dead. After that shock she saw no reason to go on fighting and surrendered Castle Rushen on 3 November 1651. She and her family were allowed to leave peacefully.

Edward Christian freed
1651

Foundation of Peel free school
1655

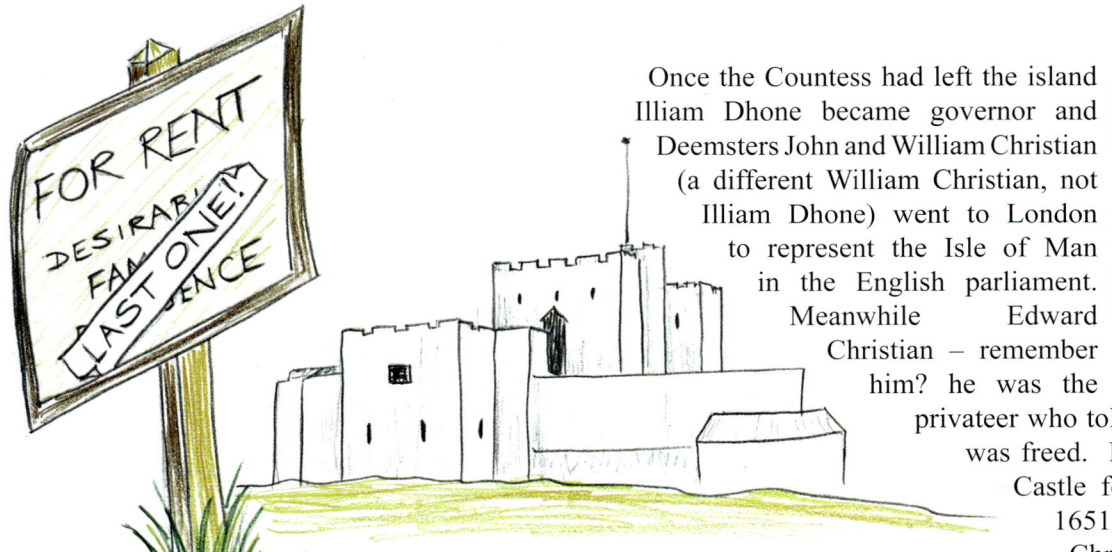

Once the Countess had left the island Illiam Dhone became governor and Deemsters John and William Christian (a different William Christian, not Illiam Dhone) went to London to represent the Isle of Man in the English parliament. Meanwhile Edward Christian – remember him? he was the privateer who told people not to pay tithes – was freed. He'd been in prison in Peel Castle for eight years. November 1651 was a good month for the Christian family.

It didn't last.

> **DID YOU KNOW?**
>
> Charlotte Stanley was the last person to surrender to parliamentary forces during the English Civil War.

... not Commonwealth – King!

People liked kings. They weren't used to being ruled by parliaments. And democracy, which is when you choose the people you want to be ruled by, hadn't really been invented yet. The head of the Commonwealth was Oliver Cromwell, top man in parliament. His title was Lord Protector, and he was so important that the Commonwealth started to be called the Protectorate. Oliver had become a sort of king. When he died he hoped that his son would take over, but people didn't like that. They wanted to go back to how things were before. They asked the old king's son to rule.

> Illiam Dhone lived from 14 April 1608 to 2 January 1663. During his lifetime:
> - Pocahontas visits London
> - The telescope is invented
> - The Pilgrim Fathers land in America
> - New Zealand is discovered
> - Galileo finds that planets go round stars
> - William Harvey discovers that blood circulates around the body
> - The Taj Mahal is built in India
> - William Shakespeare dies
> - New York is founded but called New Amsterdam

Charles II – he'd been named after his father – became king on 29 May 1660. One of the first things he wanted to do was to thank all the people who had supported him and his father. He couldn't reward James Stanley, as he'd been executed, but the king made sure that James' son, Charles Stanley, became 8th Earl of Derby and Lord of Mann.

Now, Illiam Dhone had rebelled against Charles Stanley's mother and Charles didn't like it – understandably really. He was also probably egged on by his Mum; she was

> **DID YOU KNOW?**
>
> From 1666 to 1667 Charles Stanley, Lord of Mann was also the Mayor of Liverpool.

King Charles II crowned King of England

1660

quite a forceful lady and was living at the family home in Knowsley, Liverpool. Meanwhile King Charles II didn't want to risk losing his new throne and so was trying to make sure there was peace. He made it law that no-one should be punished for fighting against him or his father Charles I. Unfortunately he didn't mention anyone who had been fighting against the Lord of Mann. Charles Stanley saw a loophole and, in 1662, arrested Illiam Dhone. He was careful though. He didn't want to get into trouble with either Tynwald or the new king. He arrested Illiam Dhone but told the Court of Tynwald to try him.

This was a worry for the Manx court. A lot of the Manx officials were related to Illiam Dhone. At the same time they didn't want to upset their new ruler, particularly after all the fighting of the last few years. Deemster John Christian was Illiam Dhone's brother and went to England to ask Charles II to tell the other Charles, Charles Stanley, that the rules against fighting the king also applied to the Lord of Mann. Meanwhile Illiam was keeping quiet.

That was a mistake. The Keys said that anyone who didn't say – loudly and several times – that he was innocent, was probably guilty. The Tynwald court found Illiam Dhone guilty of treason and sentenced him to death. Charles Stanley was delighted. On 2 January 1663 Illiam Dhone was shot by firing squad at Hango Hill. King Charles did send a message to Charles Stanley telling him that his rule about not punishing people for fighting against him also applied to Mann. Unfortunately it arrived about a week later; too late to save Illiam Dhone.

Illiam Dhone executed

1663

Religious ructions

The Commonwealth had taken religion really seriously. So seriously it had almost banned fun. Puritans, as the religious people were called, wanted to concentrate entirely on what the bible said and not be distracted by colour, or singing, or decoration. On the other hand, Charles Stanley and his family liked colour and singing and decoration. They also liked fun. (And so did a lot of other people.)

Most of the Manx kept quiet about the sort of religion they preferred and just went along with whatever the ruler said. Or if they didn't, did something else but did it secretly. Only one group didn't do what the rulers said, and didn't try to hide it. The Society of Friends. It was founded in 1648 and nicknamed Quakers in 1650 when their leader, George Fox, told them to tremble at the word of the Lord.

> George Fox was quoting from the Bible when he accidentally gave the Society of Friends their nickname:
>
> 'To this man will I look, even to him that is poor and sorry and trembles at my word.' Isaiah 66:2
>
> 'Then everyone assembled who trembled at the words of God.' Ezra 9:4
>
> Though you might have thought they'd be called Tremblers rather than Quakers…

Quakers were puritans, but weren't grumpy about it. Some puritans attacked people for believing what they did. Quakers weren't like that. In fact they loved peace, wouldn't fight anyone, and only wanted to be allowed to worship God in their own way. It's very odd, therefore, that they were the one group on the Isle of Man which everyone seemed to dislike.

It started with Illiam Dhone when he was ruling the island. He said that no-one should allow a Quaker into their house – not even another Quaker. Charles Stanley agreed and carried on punishing the Quakers after he took over. Most Quakers lived in Maughold and William Callow, who had a farm at Ballafayle, asked the Duke of York and Prince Rupert for help. The Duke of York became King James II when his brother died, and Prince Rupert was their cousin, so they were very important people. James and Rupert spoke to Charles Stanley about leaving the Quakers alone, but he ignored them – something that didn't happen very often to relations of the king. In 1665 the Quakers were sent away from the Isle of Man to Dublin or Whitehaven.

They came back though. You can't keep a good Manxman away from

> **DID YOU KNOW?**
>
> Quakers thought that families were very important and so women had a big say in what went on. They helped organise the Society of Friends and sometimes became preachers.

Quakers banished from the Isle of Man
1665

his country. Charles Stanley was annoyed but couldn't do anything about it as the king insisted it was OK. William Callow is buried in the field he gave the Quakers as a burial ground. The *Ruillic ny Quakeryn* is in Maughold just opposite the Ballafayle Cairn.

Schools start

Up until this time most children didn't go to school (stop cheering at the back there). Children were taught by their parents. A few boys who were clever or who had rich parents were taught by clergymen, as people thought that the church knew more than ordinary folk.

Philip Christian was from Peel but went to London to find work. He became rich and, when he died, paid for a school to be built and run in his home town. Philip's school was very unusual. Usually boys went to school and girls didn't. The school at Peel was open to both. Girls and boys learned different things and in different classrooms, but even the poorest children could attend.

The bishop saw what was going on in Peel and liked it. His name was Isaac Barrow and he set up a lot of other schools on the island. So did the next bishop, Henry Bridgeman, who went one better. Henry persuaded Charles Stanley – remember him? he's the island's ruler – to make it law that all children had to go to school.

Manx money

Do you get pocket money? Of course you do! And your pocket money probably arrives as metal coins and paper notes. But money is quite a new invention. People used to swap something they had for something they wanted; it's called bartering. Now that's fine for some things – bartering a bag of turnips for a couple of eggs for example – but difficult to do all the time. Imagine turning up at Shoprite with a cow on a lead to swap for groceries for the month…

DID YOU KNOW?

Children living in the other islands – Scotland, England, Wales and Ireland – didn't have to go to school for another two hundred years.

Education compulsory on the Isle of Man — 1672

Murrey's Pence made legal tender — 1679

Because bartering could get complicated people began to use tokens which represented the value of something. In Canada the Hudson's Bay Company gave fur traders a token which represented one beaver skin. The token could be exchanged for anything of the same value as one beaver skin in any of the Hudson's Bay Co. shops. As no-one else had any shops in the north of Canada, the Hudson's Bay Co. tokens were effectively the country's coins.

HALF A CHICKEN FOR A SACK OF POTATOES?! HOW MUCH?

Something very similar happened on the Isle of Mann. Not many people can say that their country's money was their own idea, but John Murrey could. He was a Douglas merchant and paid his customers in his own pennies, which he said were the same value as English pennies. The idea caught on and, in 1679, the Manx parliament made 'Murrey's pence' legal money. Murrey's pence was the official Manx money for the next thirty years. The Manx government only got around to making its own money in 1709.

The future of farming

Just like you play conkers in right season, Manxmen were farmers, fishermen and miners in the right season. They worked at farming in the spring (planting) and autumn (harvesting), fished in the summer (herring) and winter (cod) and fitted mining around everything else. Women usually did more on the farm than their husbands, brothers, sons or fathers as the men were often away fishing or mining. Farming was the most important job though, and almost everyone lived in the countryside. There were very few towns and they were very small.

For years the Manx people had been arguing with the Stanley family about who owned what Manx land – and how they owned it. That sounds odd, but even today people can't always do what they want with their own land. They can't build all over it, for example, or cut all the trees down, without the Manx government allowing it. The same sort of rules existed in the eighteenth century, but they were much more strict.

The one which really upset people was that they couldn't pass their land on to their children after they died. Farming is all about the future and farms were family businesses, but if their family wasn't going to benefit, people wondered why they should bother about fertilising crops, or mending fences to keep

St Mary's Chapel converted to Grammar School in Castletown   Manx Magna Carta
1702   1703

stock from straying. While people argued, the land got poorer and yields went down.

Neither the farmers nor James Stanley, 10th Earl of Derby and Lord of Mann, seemed able to win the argument. Eventually the bishop got involved. By this time – 1698 – Thomas Wilson had taken over as bishop. He was an ideal man to talk to both sides. Not only was he the son of a farmer, he also knew the Stanley family very well. The bishop had been the Stanley family's chaplain and James Stanley's teacher when James was a boy.

DID YOU KNOW?

The building of St Paul's Cathedral, London, England was being finished when Thomas Wilson was Bishop of Sodor and Man. The Bishop sent stone from Poyllvaaish quarry, near Castletown, to the Dean and Chapter (they run the cathedral) to make the steps up to doors of the new Cathedral.

As usual the ruler of the island wasn't living on it. It took the bishop a few years to organise things but, in 1703, he and a group of top Manxmen went across to England to talk to James. After lots more arguing James finally agreed that the Manx land really did belong to the people who farmed it. It was a very important decision and still affects ownership of Manx land today. It's known officially as the Act of Settlement but often called the Manx Magna Carta.

Tales of the tailless

Talking about farms, their cats are kept very busy catching mice and the mice's larger long-tailed cousins. Around this time people began to notice that lots of cats no longer had tails. We know that it was about this time that Manx cats started being quite common because of their name in Manx. 'Cat' in Manx is *kayt*, but 'cat with no tail' is *stubbin*. No-one invents a word for something which doesn't exist, and people started using the word *stubbin* around 1740, so there must have been quite a lot of Manx cats around by then. Any rumours that they lost their tails when they got caught in the door of the Ark, or were seized by the Stanley falcons, is just not true…

Smuggling

Smuggling didn't happen on the Isle of Man. Oh no it didn't, despite what you hear! At least it didn't 250 years ago. Those in charge like people to buy things which are made in the country where they live. If they didn't buy things made locally then local shops would close and local makers would find it harder to sell what they made – there was no internet shopping then, remember. Closing local shops is inconvenient for everyone. So governments encourage people to buy things made in their own country. Anything brought into a country from another country is 'imported'. So, if you want to import anything to sell, parliament makes you pay taxes on whatever you are importing.

James Stanley dies, James Murray 2nd Duke of Atholl becomes Lord of Man

Manx cats are common

1736

1740

Bringing things into a country costs you duty, i.e. money, and so you have to charge your customers more if you want to make a profit. People who want to buy something imported know that its price is usually higher than things made in the country.

We all know that the Isle of Man and the United Kingdom have separate parliaments. Tynwald is the Manx parliament and the Palace of Westminster runs the UK. Back in the eighteenth century the UK was running out of money. The UK parliament in Westminster decided to try to get more money by charging the people who were importing things a lot to be allowed to do their importing. The price paid by customers went up of course.

The Manx parliament didn't do this. Tynwald asked merchants to pay a small amount for its permission to import things, but not nearly so much as Westminster. Merchants paid the much lower fee, as they preferred to be allowed to land in safe harbours rather have the bother of getting things into the island secretly.

OK, so lots of luxury things like rum and chocolate and silk arrived in Mann quite legally and properly paid for. But there was far too much for the Manx to use (or buy), so the merchants moved the goods out of the big ships which had brought them from America or China or wherever, onto much smaller boats. These little boats set out from the Isle of Man to take the goods to the UK (this is called 'exporting'). But the traders didn't want to pay the very high duties demanded by the UK parliament for importing into the UK. So, somewhere out in the Irish Sea the honest little trading ships stopped being legal exporters out of Mann and started being smugglers heading for the UK.

So, as we said at the beginning, smuggling didn't happen on the Isle of Man!

Import tax

Governments like to sound important, so they use unusual words. Import tax is often called 'customs and excise'. Customs are the things you're importing, and excise is the money you pay to be allowed to import them. What you as an importer pay to the government is called 'duty'.

John Murray, 3rd Duke of Atholl becomes Lord of Man

1764

DID YOU KNOW?

Revestment means to re-invest.
Invest means to give someone something.
Revest therefore means to give something back.

Unfortunately the UK parliament noticed. Even more unfortunately the UK parliament wanted to stop it happening. And could.

The Stanley family had run out of men – sorry girls, only men could inherit – so a Scottish cousin from the Murray family had taken over ruling the island. John Murray, the 3rd Duke of Atholl and Lord of Man had a weakness. He was loyal to the king, but his father had been a traitor and his uncle had been in prison in the Tower of London. Remember, way back in 1405, the family only ruled Mann because the king said they did? Being a traitor meant that you'd gone against the king. By 1764 a lot of the king's power had been taken over by the UK parliament. The UK parliament reminded John Murray that they could take the island back. John was forced to sell.

The UK parliament passed the Isle of Man Purchase Act, known as the Act of Revestment. It paid John Murray £70,000 for the Isle of Man – what would be about a billion pounds today – and started to run the island themselves. The Manx were worried. They were right to be.

The *Peggy* was hidden in the cellar of Bridge House the Quayle family home in Castletown. Officially she was a sailing boat which carried cargo and passengers, and was built in 1789. Unofficially she was one of the Quayle family's smuggling ships. She had a new kind of keel, called a drop keel. When it was down it stopped *Peggy* moving sideways. This meant that she could use bigger sails and so go faster. The keel could also be slid upwards out of the way, so that the boat could be brought close in to shore. *Peggy* also had some small cannon to fight off revenue men; they were like a cross between water policemen and tax collectors.

Passing of the Isle of Man Purchase Act, known as the Act of Revestment

1765

CHAPTER 6

MASTERS AND MANN

So the Isle of Man was now ruled by the English king, which really meant by the English parliament. The ordinary Manx didn't like it because their (legal) trade suddenly became (illegal) smuggling, so they got poorer. The Keys didn't like it because the UK parliament started making decisions which they thought should be made by Tynwald. John Murray the ex-ruler didn't like it because he was no longer in charge. No surprises there then.

> Change of ruler – what else changed?
>
> Manx trade became more expensive.
>   UK parliament took over a lot of Tynwald decisions
>   The Manx had to pay UK taxes
>   English and not Manx became the official language

Minimal Manx

Rather like the Viking invasion, although a bit more peaceful, the Isle of Man suddenly found that a lot of foreign (English) officials had arrived to run things. Once again the invaders brought their own way of doing things and once again they had brought their own language.

English was spoken on the Isle of Man, of course, but mostly by people who had links with the islands across the water – traders, Keys, fishermen, officials. Farmers would speak less English than traders, and their wives probably wouldn't speak English at all. Everyone spoke Manx of course.

The new officials couldn't be bothered to learn Manx and, as they worked for the new ruler miles away in London, probably didn't have to. Ever played with anyone who says 'it's my ball, I make the rules'? Well, you get the idea then. Because of this new stress on everything being in English, lots of people began to learn it who hadn't bothered before. That meant that Manx began to be thought less important. It was accidental, but the Revestment Act meant that people spoke less and less Manx.

First official mail service for Isle of Man   First Manx translation of the Bible
1767   1772

44

Maximum Mail!

Something else that the new English officials hadn't realised is that the Isle of Man had no official post office. The Royal Mail was a hundred years old in England, but didn't go to the Isle of Man. Letters and parcels arrived on the island of course, but they were brought by friends and visitors, or by private carriers.

Parliament makes paperwork! The officials put up with having to arrange their own mail deliveries for a while (and grumbled about it). Eventually the UK parliament gave in and, in 1767, arranged an official mail service from Whitehaven to Douglas. They also arranged an official price, which was probably less welcome.

Obviously as the island's ruler was now the UK parliament, the post was run by the UK post office. The island had to wait another two hundred years to get one of its own.

> **DID YOU KNOW?**
>
> Stamps were not invented for another 100 years. Post in the middle of the eighteenth century was paid for by those who received it.

Tynwald takes a back seat

With UK officials running the country, and using a foreign language to do it, the Keys felt a bit left out. The UK parliament made most of the decisions and mostly ignored what Tynwald said. It was, for example, the first time that decisions made outside Tynwald had changed the amount of tax the Manx people had to pay.

The biggest thing the UK parliament wanted to change – and why it had forced John Murray to give up the island – was the smuggling. New laws, passed in the UK, now said that anyone importing anything to the Isle of Man had to pay the same amount as they did when they imported into the UK. By this new law, honest traders under Manx law, became dishonest criminals under the new UK law. Some ignored the law and carried on what was now smuggling. Some paid the new taxes. No-one was happy.

Mann made

Well, that's not quite true. A few people benefitted. The Isle of Man was counted as part of the UK (no, no, of course it isn't, but we're talking about 250 years ago). Mann, Scotland, England, Wales and Ireland were officially then all the same country. So, anyone making anything which could be sold to the islands across, could now sell things there without paying import/export taxes.

The new rules were good for miners. Mining was one of the three main jobs for Manxmen

The Great Laxey Mine started
1780

John Murray, 4th Duke of Atholl appointed Governor
1793

> **DID YOU KNOW?**
>
> A lot of lead mines also contain silver. Up until 1688, if there was a lot of silver the mine was taken over by the crown – kings at the time were always hard up. Some of the Manx mines came close to digging out enough silver to become royal mines but never actually did so. Or at least that's what their owners said...

remember (no prizes for knowing that the other two were farming and fishing). People had been digging valuable rocks called ore out of the island for over 2,000 years, but got quite serious about it in the 17- and 1800s. The copper mines at Bradda Head and Glen Chass were working by 1699. The mines in Foxdale were started before 1740 and produced lead and silver. The most famous of the lot, the Great Laxey Mine began around 1780 for zinc, lead and copper. Its huge water wheel wasn't built until 1854, as the mine wasn't deep enough to need it before then. The wheel was named Lady Isabella after the wife of the island's Governor.

It's surprising to think that the fishermen also did quite nicely out of the island's mines – and not only because many of them worked there from time to time. Quite a lot of harbours were too small for the cargo ships needed to take the ore from the mines away. Some, like the harbour at Laxey, didn't exist at all and the fishing boats were launched from the beach. The mines built bigger and better harbours for their boats and the fishing fleet benefitted.

Now, where did we leave the Keys...?

People take for granted that the Members of the House of Keys are in Tynwald because the Manx people have voted for them. But this wasn't always so. 250 years ago the House of Keys was like a club. People could only join if they were invited in by the other members. The only rules were that you had to be a man (sorry again girls) and own Manx land. You didn't even need to live on the island. John Curwen lived in Workington Hall in Cumbria, England. Around 1800 he was a Member of the House of Keys and a Member of the UK Parliament at the same time.

Once anyone became a Member of the House of Keys, they stayed a member. You could be one of the Keys for the rest of your life if you wanted to. As there were only twenty four, this meant that Keys had a lot of power.

Castle Mona built by John Murray — 1804

Point of Ayre lighthouse built; the first on Mann — 1817

The Keys might have been an important club, but they had no HQ. Sometimes they met in Castle Rushen, sometimes in the local library and occasionally in a member's house. For several years they met in the George Inn. Imagine the US Senate or the Russian Duma meeting down the local pub! Eventually things got so silly that a permanent 'home' was built for the Keys. As families do, the Keys eventually moved, but the Old House of Keys is still there in Castletown.

The Atholls are back!

John Murray the 3rd Duke of Atholl had been forced to sell the island to the UK parliament in 1765. In 1793 his son, also John, the 4th Duke was made the island's governor. The Murray family felt hard done by and still received some rent from the island, so John used his job to try and improve the family fortune. The Keys also tended to use their importance to benefit themselves and their families. No-one in charge was looking after the Manx people or their island.

Things got worse in the early 1800s. For several years the Manx harvests were bad, and, to make things worse, catches of herring were much smaller than usual. As we've said, farming, fishing and mining were the main jobs on the island, and the two most important, farming and fishing, had suddenly stopped paying very well. People had no job, no food and no future. Quite a lot of them moved across the water looking for work.

Meanwhile the Manx people left on the island were starving.

The Duke didn't notice and the Keys didn't care – many of them were exporting wheat as they could sell it for more in the UK than on the Isle of Man. It was left to the second in command, Lieutenant Governor Cornelius Smelt, to sort things out.

Cornelius had been given his job by the UK parliament and not by the Duke, so had never got on very well with his boss. He calmed the rioters down, stopped the Keys exporting wheat and kept people fed. It's not surprising that the Manx people liked him and, when he died in 1832, they decided to build a memorial in his honour. It was supposed to be a column with an urn on top. (Why an urn? No idea!) The column was built in 1837, but the money ran out so it's urn-less. You can still see it in Castletown. Locally it's called The Candlestick.

The corn riot was the last straw for Duke John Murray. He was made redundant (sacked!) by the UK parliament – they paid him to stop meddling – and died in 1830. He was the last link with a family which had ruled the Isle of Man for over four hundred years.

> The Manx liked naming their new homes after the places they'd left behind. There's a Laxey in Wisconsin, USA (appropriately it's a mining area), Tinwald in New Zealand, Mona Vale in Tasmania and even a Corlett Gardens in Johannesburg, South Africa.

Building the (now Old) House of Keys, in Castletown — 1821

William Hillary founds what becomes the RNLI — 1824

A Tiny Castle but a Mighty Tower

One of the most famous landmarks in the Isle of Man must be the Tower of Refuge. Visitors notice it when they arrive by boat. People on Douglas front get a good view of it. It appears on postcards and websites, T shirts and books. It's even lit up at night.

It was William Hillary who first 'invented' the little castle. He lived in Fort Anne, which was a large house on Douglas headland which wasn't a real fort, but looked a bit like one. He had a great view of Douglas harbour. It was much smaller then, and didn't stretch much beyond where the lifting bridge is now. At high tide Strand Street, which used to be called Sand Street, would have been underwater. In the bay, St Mary's Isle (or Conister reef as it was also called) protected the harbour from rough seas. Unfortunately the rocks were covered by water at high tide and couldn't be seen. In bad weather they might have protected the harbour but were dangerous to ships trying to reach it. From up in Fort Anne, William watched ships being battered by the sea and had also seen men drown after their ship had hit Conister rocks. He decided to do something about it.

> The Tower of Refuge got its name from a sonnet by William Wordsworth called *On Entering Douglas Bay, Isle of Man*:
>
> ...'yon Tower, whose smiles adorn
> This perilous bay, stands clear of all offence;
> Blest work it is of love and innocence,
> A Tower of refuge built for the else forlorn.'

His first idea was a lighthouse, but that seemed a bit of a waste of time. Pilots knew the rocks were there, but had trouble spotting them in bad weather. Besides it might have been confused with the harbour lights. Castles were built to keep people safe from attackers, so William built one on St Mary's Isle to keep people safe from the sea. Anyone wrecked on the rocks would be able to climb the tower and wait in safety above the waves until the storm passed. The tower had a bell so that shipwrecked people sailors could let those on shore know that they were there. To start with the tower also had a store of fresh water and food in case the wait for rescue was a long one.

William Hillary often went out in boats to help save people from drowning. In 1824 he set up the National Institution for the Preservation of Life and Property from Shipwreck. It is now called the Royal National Lifeboat Institution (RNLI).

> **DID YOU KNOW?**
>
> William Hillary couldn't swim.

Turning the Keys

The Westminster parliament and the Tynwald parliament were organised very differently. The Members of Parliament (MPs) in the UK were elected. The Members of the House of Keys (MHKs) in the Isle of Man were not.

Steam Packet Company starts	William Hillary builds Tower of Refuge	King William's College opens
1830	1832	1833

DID YOU KNOW?

James Brown of the *Isle of Man Times* was so upset with the MHKs not agreeing to being elected that he called them Don-Keys.

One MP represented a constituency and was voted in by the people who lived in that constituency. One or more MHKs represented a sheading and were given the job by the other MHKs. MPs held their job for a few years and then had to be elected again – or not. MHKs held their job for life. The Manx people looked at what was happening in the parliament across the water, and liked what they saw.

The Manx didn't like being run from another country – who would – but did like the idea of rulers chosen by the people. They wanted to be ruled by Tynwald, but wanted the members of Tynwald to be elected.

Not surprisingly, the MHKs of the time – this was the first half of the nineteenth century – didn't like the idea. Not only would they be out of a job, they wouldn't have power any more. And if they did get elected (rather than appointed), then they'd have to answer to the voters who gave them their jobs back. They were in charge and they said No. (We're back to 'it's my ball, I make the rules'…)

If someone says to you, 'no, you can't have that', you don't just accept that do you? You keep on asking and hope that someone will change their mind. So did the Manx!

Two newspapers *Mona's Herald*, and *The Isle of Man Times* led the pestering. Editors run newspapers and the editors of both the *Herald* and the *Times* ended up locked in Castle Rushen, although not at the same time. Not that that shut them up.

James Brown, Editor of The Isle of Man Times carried on making a fuss from inside his cell in the castle. He wrote lots of letters, wrote things to be published in his newspaper, and probably shouted from the windows if he had any. After seven weeks he was released as the Keys were told that they had no right to put him there in the first place.

MONA'S HERALD — RIVAL ED. IN GAOL!

ISLE OF MAN TIMES — BRAVE ED. VOWS TO FIGHT ON...

MONA'S HERALD — NO PUBLICITY SAY UNELECTED KEYS

Victoria and Albert visit Ramsey	Great Laxey Wheel, Lady Isabella built	Manx Museum founded
1847	1854	1866

Meanwhile the island's governor, Sir Henry Loch, was talking with the UK parliament about money to repair things like harbours, bridges and roads. The money had been paid in tax by the Manx people but was controlled by the UK parliament and not Tynwald. The MPs (who were elected) didn't want to give a lot of money to MHKs (who were not). They probably didn't really want to give a lot of money to anyone, but this was a good excuse. Sir Henry badgered and coaxed and eventually the UK parliament agreed to give the money back, provided that Tynwald agreed to the MHKs getting the job because people had voted for them. Governor Loch must have been *very* persuasive. The island thanked him by naming one of their steam trains after him.

> **DID YOU KNOW?**
>
> Most people think that New Zealand was the first country to allow women to vote in elections. In fact the Isle of Man allowed wealthy women the right to vote in 1881, twelve years before New Zealand did.

Exotic island

Nowadays we all travel all over the place, but at the end of the nineteenth century, most people hadn't been anywhere. Going to the Isle of Man counted as Going Abroad and people started visiting the island for their holidays.

Queen Victoria and her husband Albert were two of the first visitors, although they weren't really here on holiday. Bad weather meant that the royal yacht moored in Ramsey Bay instead of Douglas, which is why Ramsey is sometimes called Royal Ramsey. Queen Victoria stayed on board but Prince Albert came ashore and asked the first man he met, who happened to be a barber, to take him to the top of the hill so that he could admire the view. The Albert Tower was built where he stood to remind people of the royal visit.

It's difficult now to realise just how many people did come to the island on holiday. Try imagining the TT crowds (but without the motorbikes) all summer. Many of the island's most famous attractions were built for the visitors and not for the Manx. Visitors on holiday brought money to the island and were happy to spend it on having a good time.

People vote for the Keys for the first time — 1866

First railway line opened: Douglas to Peel — 1873

50

Unfortunately one of the Isle of Man banks was also quite happy to spend. Banks look after other people's money and so are supposed to be serious and reliable – even boring. This one wasn't. Dumbell's Bank loaned money to pay for a lot of things like tramways and hotels, which is the sort of thing banks do all the time. The trouble was that Dumbell's Bank didn't have enough money to pay for all the things it wanted to.

When the money ran out the bank crashed, which means it went bust and stopped being a bank. That doesn't sound too bad until you realise that banks don't have any money of their own, but use the money which belong to their customers. About half of the people on the island lost not only their savings, but all the money they had.

Imagine saving your pocket money up for a gizmo you want. You don't have enough but there aren't many gizmos left so you ask your sister, brother and granny to lend you the money, promising to pay it back out of future pocket money. Then, for some reason, you don't get any pocket money. Not only do you run out of money, but your sister, brother and granny do too. That's what it was like for half the people living on the island. People couldn't buy food as they had nothing to pay for it with. Hotels couldn't take visitors as they couldn't pay waiters and cleaners and cooks. Shops didn't open as no-one had any money to go shopping. The railways stopped running because they couldn't pay the drivers, or pay for coal – and passengers couldn't pay for tickets. A lot of things which needed money… stopped. The crash of Dumbell's Banks was a disaster for the Isle of Man.

It took a while for the Isle of Man to recover.

But it did.

Keys move from Castletown to Douglas	Yn Cheshaght Ghailechagh founded	Dumbell's Bank crashed
1879	1899	1900

51

CHAPTER 7

MANN TODAY

Remember, back in 1405, the Lord of Mann got his job providing that he gave the English king two falcons when he was crowned? In 1901 Queen Victoria died and her son became Edward VII. Strictly speaking the English ruler had been Lord of Mann since the British government bought the island back in 1765. Even so, when Edward was crowned on 9 August 1902, the Isle of Man sent two peregrine falcons to remind the new king of the old tribute.

The Isle of Man was one of the first places the new king visited. He hadn't been very well and so, like many of the people he ruled, he came to the island for a holiday. King Edward and his wife Queen Alexandra came by boat and moored in Ramsey Bay, just as the king's Mum and Dad had done over fifty years earlier. Edward and Alexandra visited Bishopscourt, Peel Castle, Cronkbourne House and Douglas before returning to Ramsey on the Manx Electric Railway.

DID YOU KNOW?

The tiny Royal Saloon that the king and queen rode in still exists and is still used. It carries the number 59.

The need for speed

Everyone knows that the TT (Tourist Trophy) races are for motorbikes, but a lot of people don't know that the TT started as a race for cars. In 1900 an international car race was started, where different countries entered national teams. Cars had only been invented in 1886 and so were only

Gaiety Theatre opens — 1900

First TT for motorbikes — 1907

52

fourteen years old, and roads were little more than cart tracks. A car race was therefore very ambitious for the time – not to say risky.

The race was planned to be held every year with the winning team in one year acting as host for the following year. Teams also had to drive cars made in their own country – a German team couldn't drive an Italian car for example. This meant that the British team had a problem. They had nowhere to test their cars! The British government didn't want to close roads, and anything like a race track hadn't been built yet. Not only did the team have nowhere to test cars, they also had nowhere to practice.

The Isle of Man is a British island and therefore counted as part of the British team, so the Isle of Man government came to the rescue. Tynwald was quite happy to close roads if it meant more visitors came to the island. So in 1904 all the British cars were tested on the Isle of Man. To be honest the Manx roads were a bit rubbish, but the island liked having the racing here so hurriedly mended them.

Motorbikes were included in the trials from 1905, and the TT race (before they'd only been practising) began in 1907. It's been on island ever since.

War

Motorcyclists were practising for the TT, but other people were practising on the Isle of Man for something a lot more serious. War. Thousands of British soldiers came to the island during the summer to train at camps at Knockaloe Mooar Farm, Peel, or Milntown, Ramsey.

Soldiers and holiday makers filled the island and, when war came in 1914, not many people took it seriously at first. Then the British government decided that the Isle of Man would make an excellent place to keep people who might be fighting against Britain. Sometimes these were enemy soldiers, and sometimes they were what were called 'enemy aliens'; 'alien' meant that

> On 28 March 1904 Tynwald agreed that road tests for the British racing team could take place on Manx roads. Trials were planned for 10 May and, of course, the necessary roads would be closed. But there was a problem.
>
> For Tynwald decisions to become Manx law they need to be read from Tynwald Hill. Tynwald Day is 5 July – and July comes after May.
>
> Tynwald got round the problem by having an extra Tynwald Day. On 5 May 1904 all the people needed – politicians, the Lieutenant Governor, Deemsters, etc. – were taken to St John's by car to read out the new law on Tynwald Hill. Almost all the people taken there had never been in a car before.

Manx old age pension starts

1920

they came from another country, while 'enemy' obviously meant that that country was fighting Britain.

Imagine if the Isle of Man were fighting Italy, for example. Any come-over who was Italian or whose parents were Italian might be a threat. They might be completely loyal to their new country of course, but no-one could be certain. To make sure that they couldn't work against Britain, enemy aliens were locked up (or 'interned') on the Isle of Man.

Of course special camps had to be arranged. The soldier training camp at Knockaloe was turned into an intern camp, but it wasn't big enough. As people didn't go on holiday during the war, hotels and holiday camps were empty, so they were used as somewhere for the enemy aliens to live. Large fences were built around the hotels so that those living there couldn't escape. The arrangements worked so well during the First World War that they were re-used for the Second.

Some internees were allowed to work on farms or help the Manx in other ways. The most famous of these was probably German archaeologist Gerhard Bersu who was interned on the Isle of Man during the Second World War. He was a history expert and spent most of the war happily discovering Manx history. It's thanks to Dr Bersu that the island knows as much as it does about its Viking past. In fact, far from wanting to escape, Gerhard and his team often asked their armed guard to help with their investigations, leaving his rifle hidden in a hedge until it was time to go back to camp.

Planes weren't used much during the First World War, but were very important in the Second. New airfields were built at Jurby and Andreas as bases for the Royal Air Force. At Andreas the church tower had to be cut in half as it was in the way of aeroplanes wanting to land.

> **DID YOU KNOW?**
>
> The people who owned the hotels which became internment camps were not allowed to stay there. Some people were only given a few days to find somewhere else to live.

Regular passenger plane service begins at Ronaldsway	Harry Kelly dies; last Manx speaker
1931	1935

Mann for the Manx!

All these changes were all very well, but the Isle of Man was still being ruled by the British government and the Manx didn't like it. The Manx National Anthem, *O Land of our Birth*, was sung for the first time at the 1907 Manx Music Festival in Peel. People wanted more of a say in what happened on their island.

As you probably remember, the Isle of Man government is called Tynwald and made up of two groups, the House of Keys (the 'lower house') and the Legislative Council (the 'upper house'). Since 1866 Members of the House of Keys (MHKs) had been elected by ordinary people who voted for them to represent different parts of the island. This is what is usually called democracy.

Members of the Legislative Council were not democratically elected and weren't even chosen by MHKs, but were given their jobs by the British government. Because of this they tended to do things the way the British government wanted, rather than think about what was best for the Isle of Man.

The MHKs did have a say in what happened, but couldn't suggest things themselves, they could only stop things happening. And they did. The UK parliament wanted to raise taxes, the Legislative Council was – of course – all in favour, but the Keys kept saying No.

The Keys used the same argument which had been first used in 1866, but they used it the other way round. In 1866 the UK parliament said that it wouldn't hand money to the Keys if they weren't elected by the Manx people. In 1919 the Keys said that they wouldn't hand money to the UK parliament if the Legislative Council didn't answer to the Manx people.

The argument worked in 1866. It worked again in 1919. From 1919, four of the six members of the Legislative Council were elected by the Keys, while the other two were appointed by the Governor. At long last the Manx people got to choose the government

DID YOU KNOW?

The first aeroplane to arrive on the island came in 1911 – by boat.

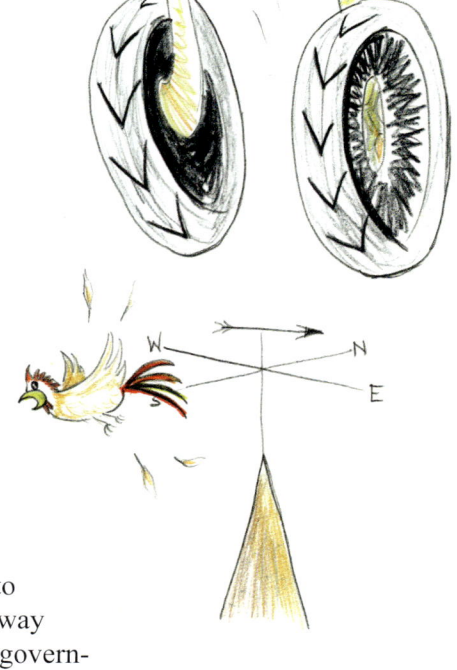

Manx National Trust starts — 1951

Manx Radio starts — 1964

they wanted, and the Manx government got to choose what happened on the Isle of Man.

More changes were made gradually and today the Isle of Man is a Crown Dependency, which means that it is not quite independent of British rule, but nearly so.

Manx laws are now made by Manx politicians for and about the Manx people on the Isle of Man. Tynwald has no official interference from anyone or anywhere else. Manx laws do still need the agreement of the Queen to be made official, but as the British ruler's permission has not been refused since 1707 – and that was in Scotland – there doesn't seem to be much to worry about.

Making money

We've said several times that most Manx jobs were in farming, fishing and mining. That's true, but a fourth job was added around about the 1870s. Tourism. More and more Manx people worked in hotels and cafés and shops and pubs serving food and drink to visitors and providing places for them to stay and things for them to buy and do. The wars stopped people going on holiday of course, but in peacetime lots of visitors came to the Isle of Man.

At least that was true until about the 1950s.

Let's be honest about this; the Isle of Man gets a lot of weather. Sun – yes – but also rain, wind, cold. And the weather changes a lot and very

First Manx stamps	Sulby reservoir opens	Manx film industry starts
1973	1983	1996

> **DID YOU KNOW?**
>
> There are only three Crown Dependencies; the other two are the Bailiwicks of Jersey and Guernsey, the Channel Islands off the west coast of France.

quickly. Many people go on holiday to enjoy the sunshine, so look for somewhere where the sun is almost sure to shine. In the middle of the twentieth century the cost of travelling became much cheaper. Ordinary people, not only those who were rich, could afford to go abroad. Spain is hot, sunny, easy to get to, and exotic. A lot of people began to go there on holiday instead of coming to the Isle of Man. Fewer visitors meant that Manx businesses which relied mainly on tourists had far less money coming in. That in turn meant that they couldn't afford to pay so many staff – or sometimes even any staff at all. People lost their jobs and the island got poorer.

There were the old staples of farming and fishing of course, but they didn't provide enough jobs for everyone. The mining had stopped with the closure of the Great Laxey Mine in 1929. The Manx government needed to try to make more money so had a think about what they could do. Today people are just as likely to work at things as different as making satellites or films, designing webpages, catering, finance or shipping. People still come to the Isle of Man on holiday of course, but not usually to sit on the beach. Visitors look at the island's history, go for walks, play golf and watch the birds. And there is always the TT.

The Isle of Man used to be ruled by its neighbours. Foreign kings fought over it, but they only really wanted the island to show off about or make money from. Now the Isle of Man rules itself, proud of its language, heritage and traditions. As the song *Mannin Veen* says:

Hroailtagh, eisht, nish gow my ghoo,
Cha vel aalid cheerey smoo,
Boayl dy vaik oo ny t'ayns shoh...

(Traveller, then, now take my word,
There is no lovelier country,
In any place than is here...)

SUMMER IN SPAIN

SUMMER IN THE ISLE OF MAN

Manx National Anthem formally adopted — 2003

Isle of Man leads Europe in space race — 2012

57

SOMETHING EXTRA

KINGS AND THINGS

Lots of people have ruled the Isle of Man, often as well as somewhere else. Below is a list of rulers of Mann, what they ruled and when.

Dates	Ruler	Country/holdings
445-452	Niall	High King of Ireland
452-463	Lóegaire	High King of Ireland
463-482	Ailill Molt	High King of Ireland
482-507	Lugaid	High King of Ireland
507-534	Muirchertach I	High King of Ireland
534-544	Tuathal Máelgarb	High King of Ireland
544-565	Diarmait I	High King of Ireland
565-566	Forggus / Domnall Ilchelgach	High Kings of Ireland
566-569	Ainmire	High King of Ireland
569-572	Báetán I / Eochaid	High Kings of Ireland
572-586	Báetán II	High King of Ireland
586-598	Áed	High King of Ireland
598-604	Áed Sláine / Colmán Rímid	High Kings of Ireland
604-612	Áed Uaridnach	High King of Ireland
612-615	Máel Cobo	High King of Ireland
615-628	Suibne Menn	High King of Ireland
616-633	Edwin	King of Northumbria
628-642	Domnall	High King of Ireland
642-654	Conall Cáel	High King of Ireland
642-658	Cellach	High King of Ireland
658-665	Diarmait II / Blathmac	High Kings of Ireland
665-671	Sechnussach	High King of Ireland
671-675	Cennfáelad	High King of Ireland
675-695	Fínsnechta Fledach	High King of Ireland
695-704	Loingsech	High King of Ireland
704-710	Congal Cenmagair	High King of Ireland
710-722	Fergal	High King of Ireland
722-724	Fogartach	High King of Ireland
724-728	Cináed	High King of Ireland
728-734	Flaithbertach	High King of Ireland
734-743	Áed Allán	High King of Ireland
743-763	Domnall Midi	High King of Ireland
763-770	Niall Frossach	High King of Ireland
770-797	Donnchad Midi	High King of Ireland
797-800	Áed Oirdnide	High King of Ireland
800-841	various Viking Jarls	
841-858	Halfdan the Black	King of Norway
858-928	Harald I, 'Fairhair'	King of Norway
928-933	Eirik I, 'Bloodaxe'	King of Norway
933-959	Haakon I, 'the Good'	King of Norway
959-974	Harald II, 'Greycloak'	King of Norway
974-994	Earl Haakan Sigurdsson	King of Norway
994-999	Olav I	King of Norway
999-1015	Earl Eirik	King of Norway
1015-1016	Earl Svein	King of Norway
1016-1028	St Olav II	King of Norway
1028-1035	Cnut, 'the Great'	King of Denmark, England and Norway
1035-1040	Harold I, 'Harefoot'	King of England
1040-1042	Harthacnut	King of England
1042-1066	St Edward, 'the Confessor'	King of England
?-1070	Godred, 'son of Sitric'	King of Mann
1070-1079	Fingal	King of Mann
1079-1088	Godred, 'Crovan'	King of Mann, Dublin, Leinster and parts of Scotland
1088-1095	Lagman	King of Mann and the Isles
1095-1098	Muirchertach II	High King of Ireland
1098-1103	Magnus III, 'Barelegs'	King of Norway, Mann and the Isles
1103-1153	Olaf I, 'the Dwarf'	King of Mann and the Isles
1153-1154	Reginald plus two brothers	Kings in Mann
1154-1158	Godred II	King of Mann and the Isles
1158-1164	Somerled	King of Argyll, Mann and the Isles
1164	Reginald	King of Mann and the Isles (for four days)
1164-1187	Godred II	King of Mann and the Isles
1188-1226	Reginald I	King of Mann and the Isles
1226-1237	Olaf II	King of Mann and the Isles
1237-1249	Harald	King of Mann and the Isles
1249	Reginald II	King of Mann and the Isles (for 24 days)
1249-1250	Harald II	King of Mann and the Isles
1250-1252	John	King of Mann and the Isles
1252-1265	Magnus IV	King of Mann and the Isles
(1263-1265	Magnus IV	King of Mann only)
1266-1286	Alexander III	King of Scotland

58

1286-1290	Margaret 'Maid of Norway'	Queen of Scotland
1290-1307	Edward I	King of England
1307-1313	Edward II	King of England
1313-1316	Robert I 'the Bruce'	King of Scotland
1317-?	Edward II	King of England
1317-1329	Robert and Edward squabbled over Mann.	
?-1329	Robert I 'the Bruce'	King of Scotland
1329-1334	Edward III	King of England
1334-1344	William Montacute	King of Mann, 1st Earl of Salisbury
1344-1393	William Montacute	Lord of the Isles of Mann and Wight, 2nd Earl of Salisbury
1393-1399	William le Scrope	King of Mann, 1st Earl of Wiltshire
1399-1405	Henry Percy	King of Mann, 1st Earl of Northumberland
1405-1414	John Stanley	King of Mann, Knight
1414-1437	John Stanley	King of Mann, Knight
1437-1459	Thomas Stanley	King of Mann, 1st Baron Stanley
1459-1504	Thomas Stanley	King of Mann, 1st Earl of Derby
1504-1521	Thomas Stanley	Lord of Mann, 2nd Earl of Derby
1521-1572	Edward Stanley	Lord of Mann, 3rd Earl of Derby
1572-1593	Henry Stanley	Lord of Mann, 4th Earl of Derby
1593-1594	Ferdinando Stanley	Lord of Mann, 5th Earl of Derby
1594-1603	Elizabeth I	Queen of England, Lord of Mann
1603-1607	James VI and I	King of Scotland and England Lord of Mann
1607-1608	Henry Howard	Lord of Mann 1st Earl of Northampton,
1608-1609	Robert Cecil	Lord of Mann 1st Earl of Salisbury
1610-1612	William Stanley	Lord of Mann, 6th Earl of Derby
1612-1627	Elizabeth Stanley	Wife of the 6th Earl
1627-1651	James Stanley	Lord of Mann, 7th Earl of Derby
1649-1660	Thomas Fairfax	Lord of Mann, 3rd Baron Fairfax
1660-1672	Charles Stanley	Lord of Mann, 8th Earl of Derby
1672-1702	William Stanley	Lord of Mann, 9th Earl of Derby
1702-1736	James Stanley	Lord of Mann, 10th Earl of Derby
1736-1764	James Murray	Lord of Mann, 2nd Duke of Atholl
1764-1765	John Murray	Lord of Mann, 3rd Duke of Atholl
1765-1820	George III	King of England, Lord of Mann
1820-1830	George IV	King of England, Lord of Mann
1830-1837	William IV	King of England, Lord of Mann
1837-1901	Victoria	Queen of England, Lord of Mann
1901-1910	Edward VII	King of England, Lord of Mann
1910-1936	George V	King of England, Lord of Mann
1936	Edward VIII	King of England, Lord of Mann
1936-1952	George VI	King of England, Lord of Mann
1952-	Elizabeth II	Queen of England, Lord of Mann

ACKNOWLEDGEMENTS

I am indebted Bob Carswell for taking time out of his busy day to help with the Manx on the blackboard on page 24. As usual this book could not have been produced without the support, encouragement and advice of my husband George Hobbs.

Thank you both for your help and assistance; any mistakes are entirely mine.

SELECTED BIBLIOGRAPHY

Cringle, Terry and others, *Here is the News*, The Manx Experience, 1992

Draskau, Jennifer Kewley, *Illiam Dhone: patriot or traitor*, Profile Books, 2012

Goodwins, Sara, *A Brief History of the Isle of Man*, Loaghtan Books, 2011

Goodwins, Sara, *A De-tailed Account of Manx Cats*, Loaghtan Books, 2013

Kermode, Philip Moore, *Manx Crosses*, Elibron Classics, 2005

Various, *A Chronicle of the 20th Century, Vols I and II*, The Manx Experience, 1999 and 2000

Williams, Gareth, *The Viking Ship*, The British Museum, 2014